A Year's Thoughts

*Collected from the Writings of William Doyle –
365 Daily Devotionals of Christian Advice for Life
and Spiritual Well-being*

By William Joseph Gabriel Doyle

PANTIANOS
CLASSICS

Published by Pantianos Classics

ISBN-13: 978-1-78987-108-1

First published in 1922

Contents

Father William Doyle, S. J.
Born March 3rd 1873.
Died, August 16th 1917.

Father William Doyle, S. J.

Born March 3rd, 1873

Died August 16th, 1917

Preface

In deference to the request of numerous readers of the life of Father William Doyle, S.J., this little book of extracts has been compiled from his letters, diaries and retreat notes. It has seemed most helpful to arrange them as a series of daily thoughts. A short title has been placed before most of the extracts.

It is, of course, to be understood that spiritual advice and resolutions are no more indiscriminately transferable than are medical prescriptions. Each reader must decide for himself how far the maxims here printed are applicable to his own case. Only those quotations which were considered to be of somewhat general utility have been selected for publication.

A. O'R.

January

1.

"A Happy New Year!" How many souls there are in want of real happiness! Poor deluded souls seeking their joys and contentment in the mocking pleasures of this world; poor sinful souls flinging themselves deeper into the mire of sin, vainly searching amid unbridled passion and unrestrained lust for the precious jewel of happiness.

A New Year! What visions of almost bound less good, hidden in the fair bosom of the new-born year, rise up before me. What treasures of grace, what innumerable opportunities of merit are within my grasp if only I seize them.

2. *A Generous Year.*

He seems to me to want a year of great devotedness, intense sympathy and passionate love from us both. Even one year of such a life would help a little, would help much to heal the wounds so many and so deep in His tender Heart. We must love Him and make Him loved more and more. He seems chiefly to ask complete abandonment to His pleasure, not lifting a finger to hinder His holy Will, but letting Him do with us exactly as He pleases.

3. *Win Your Crown.*

You say that you are convinced that God intends you to be a great saint and that you wish it ardently. He certainly has great graces prepared for you. But you must win your crown, my dear child, and draw down the eyes of His tender love by your generous per severing efforts. You have a long way to go yet. The ladder of perfection is reached but not mounted; and there is just a danger of sitting contentedly at the foot, measuring the distance to be climbed *later on* and thus putting off the day of sacrifice which Jesus asks. His Heart is opened to receive you; He points to it as your home and resting place; but the crown of thorns like a thick hedge bars the way. Are you afraid of pressing against those thorns which will wound and tear you as you force your way through? Have courage. The love of Jesus will sweeten it all, and His strong right arm will support you if you are brave.

4.

Recognise God's graces to you, and instead of thinking of yourself and your faults, try to do all you can for God, and love Him more.

5. *Christlikeness.*

Each fresh meditation on the life of our Lord impresses on me more and more the necessity of conforming my life to His in every detail, if I wish to please Him and become holy. To do something great and heroic may never come, but I can make my life heroic by faithfully and daily putting my best effort into each duty as it comes round. It seems to me I have failed to keep my resolutions because I have not acted from the motive of the love of God. Mortification, prayer, hard work, become sweet when done for the love of Jesus.

6. *The Flight into Egypt.*

Great as was the poverty of Jesus in the cave at Bethlehem, it was nothing compared to His destitution during the Flight into Egypt. Again this was voluntary and chosen and borne *propter me.*

I contrast the obedience of St. Joseph with my obedience. His so prompt, unquestioning, uncomplaining, perfect; mine given so grudgingly; perhaps exterior without interior conformity with the will of the Superior. I realise my faults in this matter, and for the future will try to practise the most perfect obedience, even and especially in little things. "An obedient man shall speak of victory." (*Proverbs* 21, 28.)

7. *Methodical Mortification.*

I think it better not to make any definite resolutions about mortification, such as "I will never do so-and-so." I know how such resolutions have fared. But I am determined to keep up a constant war against myself, now in one matter and now in another, varying the kinds of mortification as much as possible, but trying to do ten little acts each day.

8. *Quiet Prayer.*

As regards prayer, you should try to follow the attraction of the Holy Spirit, for all souls are not led by the same path. It would not be well to spend all the time in vocal prayer, there should be some meditation, thought or contemplation. Try "basking in the sun of God's love," that is, quietly kneeling before the Tabernacle, as you would sit enjoying the warm sunshine, not trying to do anything, except love Him; but realizing that, during all the time you are at His feet, more especially when dry and cold, grace is dropping down upon your soul and you are growing fast in holiness.

9. *Hard Work.*

How grand it is to be tired in working for Jesus! To lay our head on the pillow at night worn out by a hard day's work for our dear Master, with the knowledge that we have not spared ourselves, but have toiled and borne the heat and burden of the day to prove our love. A sweet, consoling thought that makes us long for the morning light to put our love to a further test.

10. *God's Children.*

"Thou sparest all because they are Thine." - *Wisdom,* 11. 27. We are all God's children, fashioned by His divine hands after His own image and likeness. From all eternity He has thought of us; before time was, we were present to His mind; and through the long ages which have passed away since first this world was made, God busied Himself with our creation, yea has longed for the hour when He could call us His children.

I am eternal in God's love. Have I always loved Him in time?

11.

The mere saving of their souls should be the last thought of religious who have vowed their lives for God's glory.

12. *Our Attitude towards our Work.*

You are bound to throw yourself heart and soul into the work God has given you to do. The devil's object is to get you so absorbed in your work, so anxious and worried about its success, that you will become, as you say, a religious only in name. However, to see his snares, as St. Ignatius calls them, is half the battle. You must go directly against what he wants. But how? First try to stir up your faith and see in everything, big and little, that happens the hand of God, remembering that He is often more glorified by our failure than by success. This will prevent irritability, and having done your best, will lessen worry, though for most of us it is impossible quite to free ourselves from that weakness. Next, a big effort, and it needs a big one at first, resolutely to give every moment to the spiritual duties and to shut out every other thought. Prayer calms the soul as nothing else can, more especially if during the day you help the grace of God by trying to keep your heart united with God, who is dwelling within your very soul. At all costs you must conquer and keep your peace of mind (after all in a few years what will it matter to any of us whether we have gained success or not?), otherwise good-bye to holiness. ...Though little acts of penance and aspirations may seem to be done mechanically, on no account should you omit them, they are far more meritorious in your present state.

13. *The Use of Imperfections.*

Are you not foolish in wishing to be free from these attacks of impatience, etc.? I know how violent they can be, since they sweep down on me at all hours without any provocation. You forget the many victories they furnish you with, the hours perhaps of hard fighting, and only fix your eyes on the little tiny word of anger, or the small fault, which is gone with one "Jesus forgive me."

14.

Jesus knows I have only one wish in this world to love Him and Him alone. For the rest He has *carte blanche* to do as He pleases in my regard. I just leave myself in His loving hands, and so have no anxiety or care, but great peace of soul. I am off now for a fortnight's spell in the trenches; and if it is not to be S. Teresa's *mori*, it will at least be *pati*.

"Take, O Lord, and receive my liberty, my health and strength, my limbs, my flesh, my blood, my very life. Do with me just as You wish; I embrace all lovingly sufferings, wounds, death if only it will glorify You one tiny bit."

15. *Union and Abandonment.*

I have been praying earnestly to know what our Lord wants from you during this year, and if I mistake not, this is His message to you. He wants a very close union with Him which you will try to effect in this way. Each morning at Holy Communion invite Jesus, with all the love and fervour you can, to enter into your heart and dwell there during the day as in a tabernacle, making of your heart a living tabernacle which will be very dear to Him....This union will be impossible without complete abandonment to God's pleasure in all the little worries of your life. Do whatever you think is most for His glory . . . and then calmly watch Him upset all and apparently bless your efforts with failure and even sins on the part of others. I have long had the feeling that your over-anxiety to keep things right or prevent uncharitableness which has caused you a good deal of worry, is not pleasing to God and prevents Him from drawing you closer in His love. *Non in commotione Dominus* [1] Labour, then, with might and main to keep your soul in peace, put an unbounded trust in His loving goodness. If you live in Jesus and Jesus in you, striving to make each little action, each morsel of food, every word of the Office, etc., an act of love to be laid at His feet as dwelling in your heart, you will certainly please Him immensely and fly to perfection.

16.

Live for the day, as you say but let it be a generous day. Have you ever tried giving God one day in which you refused Him nothing, a day of absolute generosity?

17. *Slow but Sure.*

I must warn you against the danger of wishing to go too fast or to do too much at first. You must begin humbly and build up that is, increase your penances by degrees, otherwise you might be very generous for a short time, then get tired and give up all. As a rule do not make any penance a great burden it is better to dis continue it, if it becomes such nor do anything excessive or continued very long.

18. *Worries.*

Worries? Of course; and thank God. How else are you going to be a saint? "When thou comest to the service of God, prepare thy soul for temptation," - which means trials and worries of all kinds.

If you train yourself to see God's hand in all things and rather to be glad when everything goes wrong, you will enjoy great interior peace. Here is a most important spiritual maxim for you: A soul which is not at peace and happy will never be really holy.

19.

Confession is just the one point where many, otherwise most obedient, fail to obey, with lamentable results to their own soul and perfection.

20. *The Hidden Life.*

During the reflection on the Hidden Life I got a light that here was something in which I could easily imitate our Lord and make my life resemble His. I felt a strong impulse to resolve to take up as one of the chief objects of my life the exact and thorough performance of each duty, trying to do it as Jesus would have done, with the same pure intention, exquisite exactness and fervour. To copy in all my actions walking, eating, praying Jesus, my model in the little house of Nazareth. This light was sudden, clear and strong. To do this perfectly will require constant, unflagging fervour. Will not this be part of my "hard life"?

21.

I should examine all my actions, taking Jesus as my model and example. What a vast difference between my prayer and His; between my use of time, my way of speaking, walking, dealing with others, etc., and that of the child Jesus! If I could only keep Him before my eyes always, my life would be far different from what it has been.

22.

One word about the difficulty at prayer. It is an unnatural thing, that is a supernatural thing, and hence must always be hard; for prayer takes us out of our natural element. But pray on all the same.

23.

Each look of love to the Tabernacle causes a beat of grace-laden love in the Sacred Heart.

24.

If the servant told me someone was waiting below to give me £1,000, would I say, "Do not bother me, it is too much trouble"? One little act of self-denial is more precious. Yet having let the occasion slip, I remain quite unconcerned. Should I not make a study to see how in every thing I may practise mortification?

25.

There is nothing better than the practice of aspirations, steadily growing in number. Keep a little book and enter them once a day.... I would like you to keep count of these little acts like the aspirations, but Don't go too fast; build up and do not pull down.

26. *Count - if it helps you.*

As to any practice of piety there is a double danger: recommending it as infallible, or condemning it as useless. I always make a point of saying that all things are not for all people. Characters differ so much....My own experience, and that of many others, is that the beads for marking aspirations are an invaluable help; for if there is not a definite number of acts marked or counted somehow, you will very soon find that very few are done. I think you have found the benefit of counting twenty acts of self-denial; so if you like, do the same for aspirations, increasing slowly, not too many at first and no straining.

To another Correspondent.

As regards counting the aspirations, if you really find that it is a strain on your tired head, give up the practice.

27.

What a love Jesus had for suffering: He concealed it well during most of His life, but His ruling passion broke out in the agonies of the last days on earth. Is it not, then, a mockery to call ourselves His followers if we leave Him to suffer and die alone? In urging you to be generous, I wish you at the same time to be sensible. Keep in mind these two rules. (1) If after honest trial you find anything is really injurious or hampers your work, it must be abandoned. (2) Be on your guard lest the body be too much oppressed and the spirit take harm, as says wise Ignatius. Everything is not for everyone, nor must you undertake too much in the beginning.

28.

Abandon yourself completely into the hands of God, and take directly from Him every event of life, agreeable, or disagreeable. Only then can God make you really holy.

29.

May our Beloved Lord strengthen you in your long immolation, far more painful than any martyrdom, but a thousand times more fruitful in good; the day will come, my child, when you will look back with deep gratitude to God for having chosen you to share with Him part of His Passion, when you see the glorious results which have flown from it.

30.

A kind word goes far. I stopped to say a few words to a group of men at a street corner in Kinsale, and as I walked away, I heard one of the men say to his companions: "Wasn't it kind of him to speak to us? He's a grand man entirely!"

31. *A Look Back.*

One month of the new year has passed away, leaving behind it the memory of what has been done for God and the unavailing recollection of what might have been achieved. Unavailing regret? No. For the failings and shortcomings of the month that has gone will only serve as a stimulus to a generous soul to spur him on to greater efforts in the service of his Master, efforts to use to the full the priceless gift of time, efforts to make the talents entrusted to his care bring forth the full measure of fruit and profit which our Lord will look for at His coming.

[1] "The Lord is not in the earthquake." III. Kings, 19. 11.

February

1.

I would like you to note down in a little book the following things. Every day read each item over and put a little cross after it so that you may have constantly before your mind what you have to do and your faults.

1. Number of aspirations made. Number should be increased slowly but steadily.

2. Number of acts of self-denial. Same remark; you have been going back, not forward lately.

3. Fighting against worry, anxiety, etc.

4. Patience, gentleness, sweetness with every one. This especially when you are busy, rushed, annoyed.

5. Absolute charity in words.

6. Quiet and calmness, exterior and above all interior.

7. Trying to see the hand of God in *everything* that happens to you or your work, and rejoicing in it this in your higher nature for one cannot help feeling certain things.

8. Steady persevering effort to acquire interior union with God in your soul. You would do well to read often over the Message to the Priest which I sent you.

2. *Ordinary Actions.*

It seems to me that the best and most practical resolution I can make is to determine to perform each action with the greatest perfection. This will mean a constant going against self, ever *agendo contra,* at every moment and every single day. I have a vast field to cover in my ordinary daily actions *e.g.* to say the Angelus always with the utmost attention and fervour. I feel too that Jesus asks this from me as without it there can be no real holiness.

3. *Nerves.*

I am glad you wrote to me for I, at least, can understand exactly what you are suffering; it is really a question of nerves, not of soul. You are run down like an old fiddle string, hence you can get no sweet music out of yourself, try as you may. Now, my child, Don't be troubled or uneasy, imagining God is displeased with you or that you are abusing grace. For a little while give yourself all the rest, relaxation and indulgence you can; there is to be no penance, few spiritual duties, except Mass and Communion, and you are just to do like a little child whatever your superiors tell you, read story books, etc.;

rest and riot is to be your programme just now. When the old nerves get a bit settled, you will run ahead like a giant to sanctity. I am afraid you must make up your mind for fits of depression from time to time, but that, too, will pass when you become more your old self. I shall pray for you and I know you will do the same when you get good again, but not before!

4. *Favourite Aspirations of Fr. Doyle.*

1. My Crucified Jesus, help me to crucify myself. **2.** Lord, teach me how to pray and pray always. **3.** Jesus, Thou Saint of saints, make me a saint. **4.** Blessed be God for all things. **5.** My loving Jesus within my heart unite my heart to Thee. **6.** Heart of Jesus, give me Your zeal for souls. **7.** My God, Thou art omnipotent, make me a saint.

5. *"A Martyr's Life."*

This morning I had a great struggle not to sleep. Then God rewarded me with much light and generous resolve. I was meditating on my desire to die a martyr's death for Jesus, and then asked myself if I was really in earnest, why did I not begin to die to myself, to die to my own will, the inclinations and desires of my lower nature. I wish to die a martyr's death but am I willing to live a martyr's life? To live a crucified life "seeking in all things my constant mortification"?

My God, I promise You, kneeling before the image of Your Sacred Heart, that I will do my best to lead a martyr's life by constantly denying my will and doing all that I think will please You, if You in return will grant me the grace of martyrdom.

A life of martyrdom is to be the price of a martyr's crown.

6. *Prayer and Reading.*

I would hesitate to condemn your habit of reading spiritual books, for it is an immense help to holiness, especially for one like you who has not many opportunities of hearing the word of God or getting advice. But without hesitation I would say, if you have a free hour, give half of it to a visit to the Blessed Sacrament at least as a general rule. Father Faber says: Ten minutes prayer before the Blessed Sacrament is worth an hour's prayer anywhere else. You might do some of your reading in the Chapel.

7. *Little Things.*

I am glad you have found profit from the particular examen. You must push on with this, for remember you are no beginner in the spiritual life. From time to time increase the number of acts when you find facility coming.

However it is better to keep to a fixed number steadily than to go jumping up and down, better, for example, to make twenty-five acts every day than fifty-one day and ten the next. The rule to keep before you is: Look upon nothing as too small to offer to God. Big sacrifices do not come very often, and generally we are too cowardly to make them when they do. But little ones are as plentiful as blackberries in September, and stiffen the moral courage, by the constant repetition of them, to do, in the end, even heroic things. Expect, too, that at times this steady keeping up the fixed number will pall upon you; possibly you will even pitch up the examen for a day or two, but pick it up again and no harm will be done; these failures will become fewer by degrees. Again, nothing is too small; in fact the smaller it is the better, so long as it is some denial of your will, some act you would just as soon not do.

8.

Don t be one of those who give God everything but one little corner of their heart on which they put up a notice board with the inscription: "Trespassers not allowed."

9.

Christian abnegation is not composed merely of renunciation; it leads to something tangible and definite. We abandon what is false to cling to what is true. We empty our hearts of earthly things to make room for eternal. We lose ourselves to gain Christ.

10. *Desolation.*

You seem to be a little troubled at finding yourself cold at prayer and as if our Lord had abandoned you. Were it otherwise I should feel uneasy; for this is one of the best signs that you are really pleasing to God, since He puts your fidelity to the test by sending desolation. There is no happiness to be compared to the sweets one tastes at times in prayer; but this, the greatest of all sacrifices, He will ask from you at times. Hence in darkness and dryness, when weariness and disgust come on you, when the thousand petty worries of every day crowd upon you, sursum corda, raise your eyes with a glad smile to the face of Jesus, for all is well and He is sanctifying you.

11.

The effect of fervour may be likened to that of fire on water. When cold, water is motionless and chills all that comes in contact with it, but as soon as heat is applied to it, it becomes trans formed, grows active, gives off warmth and steam, is capable of doing immense work.

12.

In thinking of health there is danger of giving in to self. I often picture St. Liguori working on hour after hour with a piece of marble pressed to his aching forehead. We must not be delicate members of a thorn-crowned Head, nor would it ever do to let poor Jesus suffer alone.

13. *Desire to be a Saint.*

When I spoke of you as a "chosen soul," or words to that effect, I did not mean to imply that you were a saint you have a long way to go yet. What I intended to imply was that I thought God had special designs on your soul and very great graces in store for you if only you will co-operate with Him in the work of your sanctification. With the record of much want of courage and generosity there is running through your life an undercurrent of earnest desire to be a saint. Not that desires alone will do the work barren desires are most dangerous to a soul, making one content with intentions only; yet without a big ardent desire nothing will be done. "If thou *wilt* be perfect," our Lord once said, implying that sanctification is largely a question of good will. This, then, is the first grace you must pray for the desire to be a saint.

14.

The merit of living under religious rule may be gathered from the difficulty of always and faith fully keeping that rule. Holiness and deliberate violation of our rules are a contradiction.

15.

We should call a man a fool who wasted his wealth warming himself before a fire made of banknotes. Do we act less madly in seeking gratification by consuming our precious day in frivolities?

16.

As the moth is attracted to the light, is drawn ever nearer to the warmth and brightness, until at length with irresistible longing it casts itself into the flame, so the Sacred Heart draws us to Itself by Its love. We are warm by the fervour of Its affection, dazzled by Its brilliancy. We come to realize the extent of that love, its foolish excesses; it bursts upon us that all this is a personal love - for *me*. Jesus has won the victory. The fluttering little moth surrenders completely and hurls itself into that furnace of love. The rest is easy. Sin ceases; imperfection becomes hateful, more hateful than former sin; a spirit of sacrifice, a longing for self-immolation springs up.

17. *Reparation.*

I saw many interesting places and things during my weeks of travel. But over all hung a big cloud of sadness, for I realised as I never did before how utterly the world has forgotten Jesus except to hate and outrage Him, the fearful, heart-rending amount of sin visible on all sides, and the vast work for souls that lies before us priests. My feelings at times are more than I can describe. The longing to make up to our dear Lord for all He is suffering is overwhelming, and I ask Him, since somehow my own heart seems indifferent to His pleading, to give me the power to do much and very much to console Him.

18. *Purgatory.*

From the cleansing fires of purgatory ascends the gentle pleading of the imprisoned souls God's own dear captives to us for help and mercy. The burning flames envelop them, but far more bitter, far more painful is the remembrance of their sinful deeds which have offended Him Whose love they now know so well. Gladly do they turn from His loving though offended gaze, and hasten to bury themselves and their shame deep in that blessed place of purifying fire. Well do they know now the foulness of sin, its black ingratitude towards their only true Friend, and gladly do they suffer now to atone for a life which was spent without love of Him.

At last the hour of their release has come. God's justice is satisfied, their souls are purified in the fiery crucible. Swiftly to the place of suffering and banishment the faithful angel guardian speeds his way. How eagerly has he longed for this hour when he may bear his loving charge safely to its home of bliss to rest for ever in the bosom of Jesus! Long ago when yet that soul was an exile on this earth has he thought of this moment. Each fresh act of virtue, each victory over temptation, gave him joy; and when that soul fell, when Satan claimed it as his own, how earnestly that angel spirit pleaded for the erring soul and won it back to grace and God.

19.

Poor God! How we creatures upset His plans! Solomon, Judas, how many spoiled saints are strewn through the centuries, lives which the world applauds, maybe, but God condemns.

20.

It is one thing to seek gratification, another to give way to feelings of satisfaction and pleasure from some high motive. A beautiful view delights me, but also raises my heart to God; consolation in prayer helps me to sacrifice and generosity.

21. *Confession.*

As regards confession it would be much better to confine yourself to the accusation of, say, three faults, and turn the whole flood of your sorrow upon these. I fear you, like so many, lay too much stress on the accusation of sins, which in these frequent confessions, is the least important part of the Sacrament. To my mind the one thing which completely changes all our notions of confession is the thought that every absolution means an immense increase of sanctifying grace or holiness. Let that be your aim and not the mere pouring out of little faults, all of which, maybe, were washed away that morning by Holy Communion.

22.

"And now I will show you what I will do to my vineyard." - *Isaiah* 5. 5. The awfulness of these words! An outraged, angry God getting ready for vengeance, telling us to watch and see the fearful evils He will bring upon the soul that has abused grace.

23.

"The power of the Most High shall over shadow thee." - *Luke* 1. 35. Light comes with this blessed overshadowing, and before God's power difficulties disappear. It is ever so. With God's grace mine, I face the difficulty and find it has vanished; I take up the heavy cross and discover it most light; I put my hand to the work and it proves easy.

24.

When you commit a fault which humbles you and for which you are really sorry, it is a gain instead of a loss.

25.

A habit of ejaculatory prayer is a sign of nearness to God, for our own holiness will be in proportion to our love and thought of Him all day long.

26.

Press on bravely and Don't mind the scratches, even when they come from human nails!

27. *Kiss His Hand.*

If He gives you only dry bread (hard crusts at that) without any butter, won't you take it in love from His Hand, and kiss the Hand that gives it? He loves your soul dearly, cling to Him, and trust Him, He so longs to be *trusted.* Be like a faithful dog at his master's feet. Have you never seen how, even after he has been punished, a really affectionate dog will come back and kiss his master's hand? Child, do this, He wants no more.

28. *Falls.*

Surely, my child, you are not surprised to find that you have broken your resolution, or rather, that the devil has gained a victory over you. I am convinced from a pretty big experience that perfection, that is sanctity, is only to be won by repeated *failures.* If you rise again after a fall, sorry for the pain given to our Lord, humbled by it, since you see better your real weakness, and determined to make another start, far more is gained than if you had gone on with out a stumble. Besides, to expect to keep any resolution, till repeated acts have made it solid in the soul, is like expecting to learn skating, for example, without ever falling. The more falls; the better (that is if you do not mind bumps), for every fall means that we have begun again, have made another effort and so have made progress. I mention this because I know that you like myself are given to discouragement and tempted to give up *all* when failure comes.

March

1. *How to keep Union with God.*

The devil will strive to spoil the bond of union between you and God, hence you must watch these things:-

1. To see in everything that happens God's doing, even if someone interferes with your work, etc., so that you will never allow yourself to be put out or annoyed in the least.

2. To crush at once every movement of impatience, that your soul may be always calm and not over-anxious about your work.

3. To be scrupulous in giving the full time to all spiritual duties; for this reason you must be up in the morning with the Community.

Write these points in your note book and read and mark their observance daily. You can show me the book when I come. Make the effort now my child, you will win a big victory.

2. *Progress.*

It is useful from time to time to pause and ask ourselves if we are, like the child Jesus, growing in wisdom and grace. Does each evening see us farther on the path of perfection, holier in the eyes of the heavenly court, more pleasing and dearer to God? When we lie down to rest, is it with the feeling that the day just passed has been one of progress in the spiritual life, of merit and victory over self? Have we crushed the promptings of self-will and trampled on our pride? Have we spent ourselves for God and wearied ourselves in works for Him? Have we been a help to the weak, the comfort of the needy, a light to the wandering one? If so, thank God for His goodness and resolve on nobler things.

3.

I did not realize you were suffering so much. You must not look upon the deepening of this state of desolation as a punishment but rather as a confirmation of the graces He has given you. He is only plunging your soul deeper into that purifying bath from which it will soon emerge dripping with choice graces and inebriated with His pure love. Trust Him, my child, He loves you too much to let harm come near you.

4. *Passio Christi.*

Passion of Christ, comfort me! Comfort me, for the day is long and weary; comfort me as I fight my way up the path of life safe to the haven of Thy Sacred Heart, comfort me in sorrow, in pain, in sickness. Comfort me when temptation rages round me and every hope seems lost, and when that last dread hour has sounded and my eyes are closing on this world of sin, Oh, Passion of Christ! comfort me then, and lead me gently to Thy wounded Sacred Feet above.

5.

All my life my study has been to avoid suffering as much as possible, to make my life a comfortable one. How unlike my Jesus I have been, who sought to suffer on every occasion for me, for me. I should be glad when pain comes and welcome it, because it makes me more like Jesus.

6.

During His Passion our Lord was bound and dragged from place to place. I have hourly opportunities of imitating Him by going cheer fully to the duty of the moment recreation when I want to be quiet, a walk when I would rather stay in my room, some unpleasant duty I did not expect, a call of charity which means great inconvenience for myself.

7. *Jesus at the Pillar.*

During all these long years Jesus has been standing bound at the pillar, while I have cruelly scourged Him by my ingratitude and neglect of my vocation. Each action carelessly done, the hours spent in sleep, each moment wasted, have been so many stripes on my Saviour's bleeding Body. He has been bearing all this to save me from His Father's just anger. And all the while I have heard His gentle voice, "My child, will you not love Me? I want your heart. I want you to strive and become a saint, to be generous with Me and refuse Me nothing." *Can* I now turn away again as before and refuse to listen?

With Jesus naked and shivering with bitter cold at the pillar, I will try joyfully to bear the effects of cold. With Jesus covered with wounds I, too, will try to endure little sufferings without relief.

8. *Dilexit me.*

The thought that Jesus has suffered so much for me to atone for my sins and past careless life in religion has filled me with a great desire to love Him in return with all my heart. I feel, too, a growing hunger and thirst for suffering and mortification, because it makes me more like to my suffering Jesus, suffering all with joy for me.

Every day has deepened my shame, sorrow and hatred for my negligent tepid life since I entered the Society, and strengthened my resolve and desire to make amends by a life of great fervour. I feel my past sinful life will be a spur for me to aim at great holiness.

9.

The greatest thirst of Jesus on the Cross was His thirst for souls. . He saw then the graces and inspirations He would give me to save souls for Him. In what way shall I correspond and con sole my Saviour?

10. *My Crucifix.*

I went on to and once more had an opportunity of a quiet prayer before the life-size crucifix in the church which I love so much. I could not remain at His feet but climbed up until both my arms were around His neck. The Figure seemed almost to live, and I think I loved Him then, for it was borne in upon me how abandoned and suffering and broken-hearted He was. It seemed to console Him when I kissed His eyes and pallid cheeks and swollen lips, and as I clung to Him I knew He had won the victory, and I gave Him all He asked.

11. *The Crown of Thorns.*

See that blood-stained crown which our sins have woven for the brows of our King! Mark the gems that glisten and gleam in that regal diadem, precious gems, priceless jewels the all-saving blood of a God made man. No earthly king had ever worn a crown like this before! Never had such a coronet marked its wearer out for the homage of his fellow men!

12.

In the Passion the light which overshadows all is the thought that our Lord, in spite of His infinite love for His Father, yet as a sinner is compelled to give Him pain, having for our sakes taken upon Himself the sins of the world. Perhaps you can see better what I mean if you picture the agony it would cause to see that all one's efforts to show love were taken as so many marks of hatred. I can understand how Jesus seems so anxious for someone "to grieve together with Him." Compassion really means "suffering with." Hence the further He leads you into the Garden of Gethsemane, the dearer will you be to Him, and the greater graces you will win for others.

13. *"Come down from the Cross."*

If I have resolved to nail myself to the cross, let me bear ever in mind that our Lord is on the other side of it. When I am tempted to come down, let me stir up my courage by recalling this scene of Calvary and resolve after the example of my Lord and Master to remain fastened to it unto death. I must beware of listening, or above all of yielding, to the universal chorus of voices which will cry out to me to come down. "Come down or you will ruin your health." "Come down and be like the rest of us." "Come down or you will render yourself unfit for your work." "Come down and walk in the beaten track." "Come down, what you are doing is an innovation and cannot be tolerated." Alas! human respect only too often does make us relax, and down we come. Or we say to our Lord, "The agony is too long or too distressing, I must have some relief; only just take out one of the nails, Lord, and give me a little respite." It is the spirit of the times to relax only a little bit, but nevertheless to relax. Ah no! I will imitate our Lord, I will live on the cross and with Him I will die on the cross.

14.

"The good shepherd giveth his life for his sheep. - S. *John* 10. 11. And you, wives and bread winners, have you no task within the fold, no little flock to tend and guard? Has not God committed to your care the innocent lambs, the little ones of your household? Within the pasture of your own family are you the good shepherd, or the thief and the hireling? ...Jesus does not ask from His shepherds now the shedding of their life-blood. But He does ask from them a death more hard, more lingering, a life-long death of sacrifice for His flock, ...the daily crucifying of every evil passion, the stamping out of sloth, of anger, of drunkenness, the constant striving after the holiness of their state of life....Look upon the great Christ, the Good Shepherd, hanging on the Cross. He is our model, our hero. Gaze well upon His bleeding wounds, His mangled limbs, that sad agony-stricken face. Look well, and pray with generous heart that He may make you in word and deed heroes in His service.

15. *Via Crucis.*

The path of life is rough and stony. Sharp flints and hidden thorns are thickly strewn upon its surface, wounding our weary feet as we toil ever on-wards and upwards towards our heavenly home. Does our courage fail, do our hearts grow faint? Do our aching eyes look sadly upon that broad and tempting way, so bright, so pleasant, so attractive to our senses but which we know would lead us on to destruction? Then turn to Christ as He hangs upon the cruel gibbet with outstretched arms and bleeding hands. *Passio Christi conforta me.* Passion of Christ strengthen me for the way is long and weary; comfort me as I fight my way along the path of life safely to the haven of Thy Sacred Heart; comfort me in that last dread hour of summons to Thy feet.

16. *Amoris Victima.*

Make this Act of Immolation to-morrow, Good Friday, at three o clock. If you mean it and try henceforth to live up to its spirit, it will be "a holocaust in the odour of sweetness," a perpetual sacrifice of your own will, ever ascend-ing before the throne of God, and will draw down upon you, I am convinced, many great and wonderful graces.

The practice of this act is simply that you give yourself into the hands of Jesus in the most absolute manner possible, abandoning especially your own will, that He may do with you, at every moment and in every way, as He pleases; you give yourself to Him as *His willing victim* to be immolated to His good pleasure, and should He so please, to be sacrificed and to suffer without complaint or murmur whatsoever He may wish.

Trials, disappointments, failure, humiliations, suffering of body and soul may crowd upon you, at least from time to time; but if you welcome them all as coming direct from His hand in answer to your generous offering, and as part of the immolation of His willing victim, you will find a sweetness and a delight in these things you never tasted before.

This is the life I promised to point out to you which, I said, would make you a greater saint than if you were buried in a cloister. For your present life is daily full of opportunities of proving that you wish and are willing to suf-fer, to be immolated and sacrificed for the love of Jesus, "the Victim of Love" who is ever offered still on our altars. Make the act in a spirit of deep humili-ty with immense trust and confidence in the grace of God which will not fail you. May our crucified Jesus take you now, my dear child, and nail you to the cross with Himself.

17. *Act of Immolation.* [1]

O most sweet Jesus, with all my heart, united to the dispositions of Your holy Mother upon Calvary, through her and with her, I offer myself to You and to the adorable Trinity, upon all the altars of the world, as a most pure oblation, uniting in myself every sacrifice and act of homage.

I offer Your Sacred Wounds and all the Blood You have shed, particularly the sweet Wound of Your Sacred Heart with the blood and water which flowed from It, and the precious tears of Your Mother.

I offer this most holy sacrifice in union with all the souls who love You in Heaven and on earth for all the intentions of Your Divine Heart, and especially as a victim of expiation and impetration on behalf of Your priests and of the souls whom You have consecrated to Yourself.

I offer myself to You to be Your *Victim* in the fullest sense of the word. I deliver to You my body, my soul, my heart, all that I have, that You may dispose of and immolate them according to Your good pleasure. Do with me as You please, without consulting my desires, my repugnances, my wishes.

I offer myself to Your Justice, to Your Sanctity, to Your Love. To Your Justice, to make reparation for my sins and those of all poor sinners. To Your Holiness, for my own sanctification and that of all souls consecrated to You, especially Your priests. To Your Love, in order that You may make of my heart a perpetual holocaust of pure love.

O Jesus! receive me now from the hands of Your most holy Mother, offer me with Yourself and immolate me along with You. I offer myself to You by her hands in order that You may unite me to Your ceaseless Immolation, and that through me and by me You may satisfy the burning desire which You have to suffer for the glory of Your Father, the salvation of souls and especially the perfection and sanctification of Your priests and Your chosen souls.

Receive and accept me, I beg of You, in spite of my great unworthiness and wretchedness. From henceforth I shall look upon all the crosses, all the sufferings, all the trials, which Your Providence has destined for me and will send me, as so many signs which will prove to me that You have accepted my humble offering. Amen.

18. *First Station.*

Around the judgement seat are grouped a motley crowd. Men and women of every rank, the high-born Jewish maiden, the rough Samaritan woman; haughty Scribes and proud Pharisees mingle with the common loafer of the great city. Hatred has united them all for one common object; hatred of One Who ever loves them and to their wild fury has only opposed acts of gentle kindness. A mighty scream goes up, a scream of fierce rage and angry fury, such a sound as only could be drawn from the very depths of hell. "Death to Him! Death to the false prophet!" He has spent His life among you doing good

Let Him die! He has healed your sick, given strength to the palsied, sight to your blind Let Him die! He has raised your dead Let death be His fate!

19. *Second Station.*

Away from the palace now a sad procession is winding. On the faces of the multitude a fiendish joy is written, they have had their wish and now issue forth to glut their eyes on the dying struggles of the suffering innocent One. Painfully He is toiling up the long narrow street, narrower still from the crowds that line the way; each step is agony, each yard of ground He covers a fresh martyrdom of ever-increasing suffering. With a refinement of cruelty His enemies have placed upon His shoulders the heavy, rough beams which will be His last painful resting place.

Cruelly the heavy beam weighs upon His mangled flesh and cuts and chafes a long, raw sore deep to the very bone.

20. *Third Station.*

Bravely has our Lord borne the galling weight of His cross; bravely has He struggled on, tottering and stumbling, longing for a moment's rest, yearning for a respite however short. But rest He will not, that He may teach us how unfalteringly we must press on to our goal. But nature will have its way. His sight grows dim; His strength fails and with a crash our Saviour lies extended on the ground. Oh! if you have not hearts of stone let Him lie even thus, poor, crushed and broken thing. If you have but one spark of compassion left, one tender feeling of sympathy urge Him not on awhile, so spent, so weary. On a poor maimed brute you have pity think of the sorrow of Him extended there.

21. *Fourth Station.*

To sensitive souls the pain they cause others is far worse than any sufferings they may endure themselves. They may have much to endure, but to see others in pain causes them deeper grief. Jesus and Mary meet. Alone He could have suffered with joy so that she, His dearest Mother, might have been spared the agony of seeing all He must endure. With one look of pity Jesus reads the anguish of that cruelly lacerated heart; with one long gaze of infinite love and pity Mary sees the depth of her Son's woe, His long hours of torture, His utter weariness, His sorrow, His grief, His anguish. May she not help Him? at least lift for one moment that cross?

22. *Fifth Station.*

When God lays a cross upon us, some mis fortune, some unexpected burden, instead of thanking Him for this precious gift, too often we rebel against

His will. We forget that our Saviour never sends a cross alone, but ever sweetens its bitterness, lightens its weight by His all-powerful grace. With reluctance, with unwillingness, Simon bears the cross of His Master. At first his spirit revolted against this injustice, his pride rebelled against this ignominy. But once he accepted with resignation, his soul was filled with heavenly sweetness, he felt not the weight of the heavy beams, he heeded not the jibes of the multitude but pressed on after His Master, proud to be His follower.

23. *Sixth Station.*

As the sorrowful procession moves slowly on, a woman, who with anxious gaze has watched its approach, steps forward and wipes the sacred face of Jesus. It is a simple action, yet reveals the kindly thoughtfulness of a charitable heart. Gladly would Veronica have done all in her power to lessen the sufferings of the Lord, to ease the dreadful burden which was crushing Him, to show some mark of sympathy and com passion. That little act of love touched the broken Heart of Jesus; He wipes the clotted blood and streaming sweat from His Face, leaving His sacred image stamped on the veil of Veronica; but deeper and more clear cut did He impress on her heart the memory of His passion.

24. *Seventh Station.*

Jesus falls a second time, crushed beneath the weight of His awful sufferings which are fast draining His strength. Exhausted and spent He lies upon the rough-paved ground, a cruel resting place for His bleeding, lacerated body. Vainly He tries to rise, for love impels Him on to the consummation of the sacrifice, but His tottering limbs will not support Him and once again He falls upon the ground. Again the soldiers with fiendish brutality drag Him to His feet with coarse jibes and mocking laughter, with kicks and blows they drive Him on, pulling Him now forward, now back, striving if possible to add to the sufferings of the patient victim.

25. *Eighth Station.*

The disciples of Jesus have deserted their Master, and fearful for their own safety, have abandoned Him to His fate. Peter who would die for Him, Matthew who left all to follow Him, are far from Him now and dread to be pointed to as His friends. Yet Jesus is not alone. A few, a faithful few, remain beside Him still, poor, weak women, but strong with the courage of love. The brutal crowd surge round, inflamed with hate and lust for blood; but they offer Him the tribute of a woman's heart the silent tears of sympathy.

"Weep not for Me," He says, "weep rather for those who unlike these My executioners will one day crucify Me again with full knowledge of what they do."

26. *Ninth Station.*

The hill of Calvary is almost reached, the hour of the great sacrifice is at hand. Still the heart of Jesus thirsts for suffering to show His great, His all devouring love for us. Again He falls! With limbs all bruised and broken, with a body all one raw, red, quivering sore, each step He took was agony. But to fall thus helpless on the ragged ground, to be kicked and beaten as He lay with nerveless limbs all paralyzed with pain must have been to His high-strung, delicate frame a thousand-fold martyrdom. The executioners were alarmed. Was death going to rob them of their victim and cheat them of the joy they promised themselves as their victim writhed in the agonies of death?

27. *Tenth Station.*

At last He stands upon the hill of shame to pay the price of our redemption. In the eyes of His Eternal Father, a sinner laden with the crimes of a wicked world; before men, the most abject and abandoned of creatures. A brutal soldier advances. He lays his hand upon the garment of Jesus and roughly tears it from His sacred shoulders. The cloth has sunk deeply into the gaping wounds left by the recent scourging, and driven deeper still by the weight of the cross and the oft-repeated blows. With a horrid, rending sound the wounds are torn open afresh, the sacred blood gushes forth anew and bathes His limbs in its ruddy stream. It is a moment of awful agony.

28. *Eleventh Station.*

Upon His last resting place Jesus lays Himself down. No soft bed, no easy couch to ease the agony of His aching limbs, but a hard, rough beam must be His place of death. Meekly He extends His arms, those arms ever open to welcome back the repentant sinner, and offers His hands to be pierced as the Prophet had foretold. A long, blunt nail is placed upon the palm: a heavy, dull thud, the crunch of parting flesh and rending muscle, the spouting crimson blood which covers the face and hands of the hardened soldier and Jesus is fastened to the cross. Come, sinner, gaze upon your work for you have nailed Him there! Your sins it was which flung your Saviour down, your sins which drove the iron deep into His sacred flesh.

29. *Twelfth Station.*

Upon the cross He hangs now, the most abject and despised of all men, the butt for vile jests, a common mark for all to hurl their jibes at. There He hangs, in agony no human lips can tell, no mind conceive, an impostor, a vile hypocrite, a failure. "He came to make Himself a King! See, we have crowned

His brow with a royal, sparkling diadem. He sought a kingdom! From that elevated throne let Him look upon the land which will never be His now. He threatened our Scribes with woes and punishments, let Him look to His own fate and if He has that power which some say was His, let Him come down now from the cross and we too shall believe in His word."

30. *Thirteenth Station.*

Mary stands at the foot of the cross to receive in her arms the lifeless body of her Son. Once more His head is resting on her bosom as it used to do long years ago when a little child He nestled to His Mother's breast. But now that sacred head is bruised and swollen, stamped with the cruel mark of the mocking diadem; His hair all clotted with the oozing blood, tangled and in disorder. Even she, upon whose heart is stamped every lineament of her Son's dear face, can scarcely recognise His features now. On every line is marked the anguish of long drawn agony, of torture and agonizing pain, of woe, unutterable woe, of sorrow, suffering and abandonment.

31. *Fourteenth Station.*

The final scene of the awful tragedy is drawing to a close. Reverently the faithful few bear the dead Christ down the hill of shame, that body from which all the care of loving hands cannot remove the marks of the cruel scourge, the rending nails, the lance's gaping thrust. Into the tomb they bear Him, the burial place of a stranger, best suited to Him Who during His life had not where to lay His head. Reverently they lay Him down; one last, fond embrace of His own Mother before they lead her hence, and then in silence and in sorrow they leave Him, their dearest Master, to the watchful care of God's own angels. Sin has done its work! Sin has triumphed, but its very triumph will prove its own undoing.

[1] Some of the sentences in this Act of Immolation are taken from Souer Gertrude-Marie Legueu, - *Une mystique de nos jours,* p. 145 (abridged Eng. trans., p. 25).

April

1. *"What must I do to become a Saint?"*

1. Excite in myself an ardent desire and determination to become one, cost what it may.
2. Beg and pray without ceasing for this grace and the desire of holiness. 3. Take each action and duty as if it were the last and the only one of my life, and perform it with extraordinary fervour.

4. Have a fixed duty for each moment and not depart from it; never waste a moment.

5. The spirit of constant prayer.

6. Relentless war against my will and inclination; *agere contra* at every moment in all things.

7. The faithful practice of little mortifications.

2.

May every Easter blessing be yours, and may our crucified Jesus, Who has certainly drawn you to Him on the cross, raise you up now in the glory of His Resurrection.

These words have been ringing in my ears this morning, "Ought not Christ to have suffered these things and so to enter into His glory?" - *Luke* 24. 26. If there had been another road, He, whose tender Heart ever shrank from inflicting pain, would gladly have pointed it out to His followers, but there is none other if we wish to reach heaven and certainly none other to find His love. But why should I speak to you of suffering on this morning of joy? I do not know except that I feel Jesus would have you always stand with arms opened wide to embrace the cross, and even to draw it to your bosom, as the Swiss patriot gathered the spears of his country's enemies into his breast.

3.

If one of two has to suffer, why shouldn't you be the one? Always choose the worst and the hardest. Do not try to get rid of what is troublesome or annoying, but hold on to it. The cross is a treasure.

4.

Whenever there is a question of choice, ask yourself, "Which would please God most?" then, "Which will come hardest to my nature?" It is this then that you will choose; and even though you may not always do so, keep your mind and will bent in the direction of doing always whatever goes against self. This is true holiness.

5. *Little Slips.*

You must not mind these little slips for they are nothing else but look up at Him who knows and understands everything, and simply say, "I do trust You." Depend more on God. You cannot become holy, you cannot overcome your faults; but Jesus can give you help, strength and courage, and bring you at length to a high degree of perfection.

You are not trusting Him enough. Do stop worrying and leave this whole matter in His hands. This is only a trick of the devil to disturb your peace of soul; and without peace there can be no prayer, no union with God, no work done purely for Him. Put this into mortification of your thoughts and work away at conquering it.

6.

From the Tabernacle Jesus seems to say, "Stay with Me for it is towards evening and the day is now far spent." This should urge me to come to visit Him often.

If my resurrection is a real one and is to produce fruit, it must be external, so that all may see I am not the same man, that my life is changed in Christ.

7.

The example of men of the Third Class [1] in the world should shame me. What determination, what prolonged effort, what deadly earnestness, in the man who has determined to succeed in his profession! No sacrifice is too great for him, he wants to succeed, he will succeed. My desire, so far, to be a saint is only the desire of the man of the First Class. It gratifies my pride, but I make no real progress in perfection I do not really will it.

8. *Grace.*

I wish I could write to you at length about grace. It is a fascinating subject. You are quite right in calling it "a participation of the divine nature," since Scripture uses almost the same words to describe it. A comparison of the Fathers of the Church helps to explain things a little. A piece of iron, they say, placed in a fire does not in reality change its nature, yet it seems to do so; it burns and glows like the fire around it, it cannot be distinguished from the fire. In similar wise a soul clad in grace borrows beauty and magnificence from God's beauty and magnificence; it seems to partake of the nature of God. What joy to remember that every tiny thing done for God, an act, a word, a glance even, brings fresh grace to the soul, makes it partake more and more of the nature of God, until St. Paul has to exclaim: "I have said you are gods!" and no longer mortals. Our Lord longs for this transformation, and so He sends many hard trials to hasten the day of this perfect union. Let Him, then, have His way. You can have perfect confidence that He is doing the right thing ever and always. Holiness is really nothing more than perfect conformity to God's Will, and so every step in this direction must please Him immensely.

9.

If you are not yet strong enough to seek humiliations, just accept the little reverses that come. When you say or do awkward things, give them to our Lord and tell Him you are glad of them. Say: "All these are humiliations, so they *must* be good for me."

10.

I want you to stick to two things: the aspirations and the tiny acts of self - conquest. Count them and mark them *daily.* You need nothing else to make you a saint. The weekly total, growing bigger as you persevere, will show you how fast you are growing in perfection.

11. *Dryness.*

You seemed to be troubled that you cannot love God when trials come and all is darkness. But that is just the moment when you love Him most and prove your love the best. If only, when you are in desolation and dryness, you *force* yourself to utter an act of love or an oblation of yourself without a particle of feeling, you make an offering which is of surpassing value in His eyes and most pleasing to His Sacred Heart. A dry act of love is a real act of love, since it is all for Jesus and nothing for self. Therefore welcome the hard black days as real harvest time.

12.

How sweet it is when our day is ended to find the body tired, the head heavy and jaded with work done for Jesus. The day has been a long one, bearing to us more than its share of disagreeable duties and unpleasant tasks; un expected troubles have met us ... but through it all we have unflinchingly plodded on, doing the Master's work for love of Him.

13.

How few of us can look back upon the past and not wish to recall many of the days that are gone! Age brings wisdom in its train, but alas! how often does that wisdom come too late. Youth with its golden promise has passed and left us with the promise unfulfilled, the bright hopes unrealised. While yet that heart was fresh and young, life held out to it many a noble ambition; the pinnacle of fame was steep, but hope and youth and courage would win its dizzy summit. No unnoble aim would be its goal; ever onward, ever upward, striving after higher, nobler things. Did he reach the promised shore? Or did some ignoble passion drag him down to mock at his disgrace, to glory in his broken hopes, to chide and taunt him with the vision of a wasted life and blighted hopes?

14. *Expect Falls.*

You seem to have been going through a harder time than usual lately, and this evidently has come as a surprise to you. But is it not the best of signs that all is well, that God has accepted your generous offer to bear all He wishes to send you, and that the devil is furious and alarmed at the progress you have made in perfection and mad at the harm you have done to his evil cause? The storm has come upon you, and you, foolish child as you always were, have thought all is lost because you have bent a little like the reed before the wind. No, the want of courage and firmness and generosity will only serve to tumble and throw you the more confidently into the strengthening arms of our dear Lord, since it makes you see that without Him you can do nothing.

God always seems to permit this to happen even to His saints. I read recently in the life of a holy soul who had promised to give our Lord all: "Three times to-day I *deliberately* avoided a humiliation and a little act of self-denial." Hurrah, boys! I say; if the saints act like that, there is some hope for you and me. If there has been any falling oft in your generous resolution, go back humbly to the feet of Jesus now, and take up bravely the cross which means so much for His glory and your happiness.

15.

If I were put in a dungeon, like the martyrs, with nothing to lie on but the bare stone floor, with no protection from intense cold, bread and water once a day for food, with no home comfort whatever, I could endure all that for years and gladly for the love of Jesus; yet I am unwilling to suffer a little inconvenience now, I must have every comfort, warm clothes, fire, food as agree able as I possibly can, etc.

16.

Sanctity is so precious, it is worth paying any price for it. God sanctifies souls in many ways, the path of daily and hourly sacrifices in *everything* and *always* is mine.

Can a Jesuit, who deliberately refuses his Lord any act of self-denial, which he knows is asked from him, ever be really *insignis*? Will Jesus be content with only half-measures from me? I feel He will not; He asks for all. My Jesus, with Your help I will give You all.

I was greatly struck with the thought that at His birth, our Lord began a voluntary life of suffering which would never end till He died in agony on the cross. *All this for me!*

17.

Hunt down and slay your *little* faults. Nothing hinders the free and generous action of the Holy Spirit more than these.

18.

"They forgot God who saved them." - *Psalm* 105, 21. To how many may not these words be applied to-day! How many there are who come into this world and pass beyond its bounds and never know the loving God who died to save them. How many souls, even Christ's favoured ones, think not of the bitter woe and deepest pain which He, who shed His precious Blood for man's redemption, endured that they might live.

19. *"Holy Follies" not asked from us.*

What is it to be a saint? Does it mean that we must macerate this flesh of ours with cruel austerities, such as we read of in the life-story of some of God's great heroes? Does it mean the bloody scourge, the painful vigil and sleepless night, that crucifying of the flesh in even its most innocent enjoyment? No, no, the hand of God does not lead us all by that stern path of awful heroism to our reward above. He does not ask from all of us the holy thirst for suffering, in its highest form, of a Teresa or a Catherine of Siena. But sweetly and gently would He lead us along the way of holiness by our constant un swerving faithfulness to our duty, duty accepted, duty done for His dear sake. How many alas! who might be saints are now leading lives of indifferent virtue, because they have deluded themselves with the thought that they have no strength to bear the "holy follies" of the saints.

How many a fair flower of innocence, which God had destined to bloom in dazzling holiness, has faded and withered beneath the chill blast of a fear of suffering never asked from it.

20. *Devotion to the Holy Ghost.*

I sometimes think we lose very much by not having more devotion to the Holy Ghost. After all He is the Dispenser of the very things we need to make us saints. Invoke Him frequently, and don t forget that Fr. Faber sums up devotion to the Holy Spirit as "a constant docility to His inspirations." The inspiration He will send to you most often, if I mistake not, will be His desire for the absolute sacrifice of your will to His, so that in time there should not be even interior rebellion against what He wishes. This Promised Land may still be afar, but God will help you wonderfully if you set out bravely to reach it.

21.

This morning I lay awake powerless to over come myself and to make my promised visit to the chapel. Then I felt prompted to pray; I said five aspirations and rose without difficulty. How many victories I could win by this easy and powerful weapon!

22.

Great light at meditation on the value of one aspiration. If I knew I should receive £1 for each one I made, I would not waste a spare moment. And yet I get infinitely more than this, though I often fail to realise it.

23.

It ought to encourage you to feel the desire for penance growing in your soul. After all is it not a mockery to call ourselves the spouses of a *crucified* Love if our lives are not to some extent crucified also? You need to be careful in the matter of privation of sleep more than in other things, but let there be no limit to interior mortification.

24. *Patience with Oneself.*

I think there is no harder trial in the spiritual life than the one you speak of. One feels so weary of it all, fighting and struggling against things which seem so small and mean, and where there is apparently so little merit to be gained, and then comes the longing to throw it all up and be content with just doing the bare necessary to save one's soul. You must have great patience with *yourself,* my dear child, and not expect to get into a region of perfect peace where there would be no trials or worries or fighting against self even the saints did not enjoy that calm.

Remember, God sees the intention, which in your case is generous and unreserved. He is quite pleased with that, and only smiles when He sees us failing in our resolve and determination to be perfect. To console you, here is the confession of the great Saint Teresa [2]: "The devil sends me so offensive a spirit of bad temper that at times I think I could eat people up." She was canonised, so there is some hope of salvation for us yet.

25. *"Ginger-Beer" Fervour.*

No one is holy who is not fervent. But the fervour of the holy is not an impetuous, novitiate first-fervour, which does not and cannot last; it is not a fervour that multiplies resolutions and piles up pious practices that bow one to the ground in disgust and despair; it is not a fizzling "ginger-beer" fervour that disappears as soon as it appears, but "an ardent zeal inspired by reason in the accomplishment of duty."

26.

God sometimes seems to ask the impossible, a sorrow, a cross. Oh! it would crush me! How can this be? How? Lord, I do not know how, but You do. I will trust You always.

27.

To many God gives not only the great grace of a religious vocation, but also another wonderful grace. This is the grace of Second Conversion, by which we are invited to give ourselves entirely to God. If this grace be not received in vain, we may even at the eleventh hour come to the practice of the most heroic sanctity, refusing God *nothing.*

28. *A Loving Crucifixion.*

Over and over again I asked myself, when reading that book, was it not strange that I should come across the very ideas which had been in my mind so long: namely, the longing of our Lord for more souls who would be absolutely at His mercy, His pleasure and disposal; souls in whom He could work at will, knowing that they would never resist Him, even by praying to Him to lessen the trials He was sending; souls who were willing and longing to be sacrificed and immolated in spite of all the shrinking of weak human nature.

Now I have long thought He wants that from you. And everything that is happening seems to point that way. If you make such a surrender of yourself absolutely into His hands, I know not what humiliations, trials and even sufferings may come upon you, though you must not ask for them. But He will send you grace in abundance to bear them, He will draw immense glory out of your loving crucifixion, and in spite of yourself He will make you a saint...This must be chiefly an act of the will, for it would be unnatural not to feel trials or humiliations; but even when the tears of pain are falling, the higher nature can rejoice. You can see this is high perfection, but it will bring great peace to your soul. Our Lord will take the work of your sanctification into His own hands, if you keep the words of the *Imitation* (iii. 17. 1) ever before you: "Child, suffer Me to do with thee whatever I will." Do not be afraid for He would not ask this if He did not intend to find you the grace.

29.

A mother puts her little child on its feet, but the child itself must do something, must make an effort if it wants to walk. God does all that is necessary, but man must do his share.

30.

If God tries you in the way you speak of, all eternity will not be long enough to thank Him for such a grace. It will mean so much for your sanctification. But I am inclined to think this will not come yet. God is only asking whether you are ready for that crucifixion. Do not pray for it, but offer yourself, as you have done, humbly, bravely and with great trust in Him, for the cross never comes alone, it always brings its grace.

I will ask Jesus in the morning, when I hold Him in my hands, to give you a brave heart, and to support and comfort you when the hour of trial comes.

[1] See "The Three Classes" in the Spiritual Exercise of S. Ignatius.
[2] Life, 30. 15.

May

1. *Interior Union.*

I feel drawn still more the life of "interior union." To acquire this I must practise the following: -
1. Constant and profound recollection. **2.** To keep my thoughts always, if possible, centred on Jesus in my heart. **3.** To avoid worry or anxiety about future things. **4.** To avoid useless conversation. **5.** Great guard over my eyes, not reading or looking at useless things.

2. *Mother of Mercy.*

"Mother of Mercy!" What words more sweet in the sinner's ear! The past has been a long record of sin and sinfulness, of grace abused and calls neglected. God's inspirations have been despised, His patience abused, His anger defied. In terror the soul looks back on a mis-spent life; in horror it thinks of a judgement, just and searching, to come. How face the look of an angry God? How stand before Him to whom nothing is hidden? How answer for the days and years squandered which were given to serve Him alone? Oh! turn then, poor soul, and look to Mary. Look to her who is all merciful that she may obtain for you pardon and mercy. She is kind and loving; she has a mother's heart full of pity for the erring, a Mother of Mercy to the sinner and the fallen.

3. *The Heroism of the Humdrum.*

At the community Mass this morning *I again felt an overpowering desire to become a saint.* It came suddenly, filling my soul with consolation. Surely God has an object in inspiring me so often with this desire, and has great graces for me if I will only cooperate with Him.

Reflecting on this inspiration afterwards, I saw more clearly that the chief thing God wants from me at present is an extraordinary and exquisite perfection in every little thing I do, even the odd Hail Marys of the day; that each day there must be some improvement in the fervour, the purity of intention, the exactness with which I do things, that in this will chiefly lie my sanctification as it sanctified St. John Berchmans. I see here a vast field for work and an endless service of mortification. To keep faithfully to this resolve will require heroism, so that day after day I may not flag in the fervour of my service of the good God.

4. *The Narrow Path.*

Don t shrink from the narrow way God has pointed out to you so often and so clearly. You can never be the Spouse of the Crucified unless you are willing and ready for crucifixion; and the more this generous spirit springs up in your heart, the nearer and dearer will you be to Jesus. Love for Love. Blood for Blood. Life for Life. Will you give Him all? What do the sacrifices of the past cost you now? The future may never come, and so you have only the suffering of the moment to bear for His dear sake.

5. *God's Presence.*

All day long keep Jesus close beside you with a thought, with a word, with a look, a smile, so that you may verify the words of General de Sonis, "I did not lose sight of the presence of God for one half -minute during the battle."

6. *Self-Conquest.*

I must thank you for your kind letter and the basket of "flowers," which had a delicious perfume; though I missed one flower from the basket, the purple passion-flower of acts of self-conquest, the one thing which makes religious life a paradise from the interior joy they always bring. Though I Don't practise what I preach, I have urged this during retreats in season and out of season; and many who have generously taken it up have told me it has made them "fly to God."

Two little rules will help you to get this spirit: (1) the advice of A Kempis, "Seek always to do the will of another rather than your own "; (2) train yourself to say no to your yes and yes to your no.

7.

Try to get down low and follow out what He Himself taught: "Unless you become as little children." This will make you more confiding, more trustful and more naturally loving, which sometimes we are not, our love for Him being much too formal and prim.

8. *The Path of Dryness.*

I am quite convinced our Blessed Lord is well pleased with you and will become more so if you walk bravely along the path He has chosen for you in His love, the path of dryness and little sensible consolation. You may find it hard to believe me when I say you must be very dear to Him and very pleasing in His sight, since He has marked you out for this trial. Mind, it is not a punishment for past infidelity, but a special grace reserved for the few. The only danger comes from the temptation of the devil, that God has abandoned you and it would be better to chuck it all up. He will beat you in the fight at times, making you weary of this never-ending war against self and forcing you to yield to nature. But no harm is done provided you *start again.*

9.

We love our life, cling to it, hug it, study how to prolong it, rebel if God thinks fit to shorten its span, nay, when we have run our scriptural appointed course "three score and ten, and what is more of them is labour and sorrow" Psalm 89 we hunger for more. But do we ever seriously ask ourselves, Does this life carry any responsibility with it?

10. *God in our Heart.*

I think our Lord wants your whole day to be one continued act of love and union with Him *in your heart,* which has no need of words to express it. Your attitude ought to be that of the mother beside the cot of her babe, lost in love and tenderness, but saying nothing, just letting the heart speak, though the wee one cannot know it as Jesus does. There is nothing more sanctifying than this life, which few, I fear, reach to, since it means a constant effort to bring back our wandering imagination.

11. *"Sink into God."*

By all means follow the guidance of the Holy Spirit and do not bind yourself to anything which you find a hindrance. Just let yourself "sink into God" when in His presence. Don't try to pray in words, but love Him which, of course, is the highest prayer and then abandon yourself to His pleasure, whether that be con solation or darkness. ... In the matter of prayer always try to follow the attraction of the Holy Spirit. Since you find spiritual Communions such a help, keep to them. There is no surer means of great grace, since we can repeat these Communions a thousand times in the day, and, says S. Thomas, "get often more grace than by our sacramental ones." ...Try to keep our divine Lord company in your heart all day long, thinking of Him within you a union which will bring you many graces and make His presence much more real.

12. *Give All.*

Every time I see a picture of the crucifixion or a cross, I feel strangely affected and drawn to the life of immolation in a strange way. The heroism of Jesus appeals to me; His "naked crucifixion" calls to me and it gives me great consolation and peace to offer myself to Him on the cross for this perpetual living crucifixion. How often does He not seem to say to me in prayer, "I would have you strip yourself of all things every tiny particle of self-indulgence, and this ever and always? Give Me *all* and I will make you a great saint." This then is the price of my life long yearning for sanctification. O Jesus, I am so weak, help me to give You all and to do it *now.*

13. *That Feeling of "Being Crushed."*

You will see, therefore, that your present state is quite a natural one to expect, and instead of depressing you, should rather console and rejoice your heart. Do not be surprised if you find the life of sacrifice, constant sacrifice, a hard one. Crucifixion is ever so to human nature, even the big saints found that, and shrank from it with all their might. Poor weak human nature is ever crying, "Come down from the Cross," and the devils, of course, will pull us down if they can; the easier life of others, too, is a temptation to us and is naturally more attractive; all of which often plunges one into a feeling of sadness and that feeling of "being crushed," about which you speak.

14.

It depends entirely on myself whether I become a saint or not. If I *wish* and *will* to be one, half the battle is over. Certainly God's help is secured. Every fresh effort to become holy gets fresh grace, and grace is what makes the soul holy and pleasing to God.

15.

God has work for each one to do; the devil also. For each one can be an influence for good or evil to those around. No one goes to heaven or hell alone. Unless I am holy, I may do the devil's work. The closer I try to imitate the Sacred Heart, the holier shall I become. How can I get nearer that Divine Heart than by receiving Holy Communion often and fervently? The Sacred Heart will then be next my own and will teach me quickest and best how to be a saint.

16. *No Selfish Moping.*

Are you weary of the fight already and willing to give in to the enemy? Never mind, come back, begin again, Jesus wants you. There are millions of pagans to be saved, a hundred thousand dying sinners every day to be rescued. For shame, to sit down and cry over your own self and troubles while so many others need your aid. Ask your holy patron to help you. Don't lose heart. I think I can understand better than many what you suffer. I am not angry with you why should I be when I know how sorely you are tempted and the rage of the devil against you? But I certainly shall be angry if you play the coward and admit that you are beaten.

17. *A Visit to the Blessed Sacrament.*

Do we realise the infinite possibilities of grace which lie hidden in the Tabernacle? Jesus only awaits our coming; and even before we have begun to beg His help, He has opened the treasures of His Sacred Heart and filled our hands with priceless gifts. What monarch ever rewarded his subjects as Jesus repays us for the little trouble it costs us to visit Him even for one short moment.

18. *Joy of Spirit.*

"The just shall rejoice in the Lord." - *Psalm* 63, 11. If there is any certain mark of the abiding presence of the Holy Ghost in the soul, if there is any visible pledge of future happiness destined for man, assuredly it is lightness of heart and joy of spirit. On some souls the black clouds of despondency and gloom never settle, sorrow may touch them with her sable wings, grief may blanch the hair and early care rob the step of its youthful spring; but the joy which is not of this earth ever shines upon the brow of such a soul, and the heavenly peace and calm within shine brighter through the flood of tears which are wrung from a sore-stricken heart.

19. *God's Loving Refusals.*

How often have we murmured against the good God because He has refused our petitions or frustrated our plans. Can we look into the future as God can do? Can we see now and realize to the full the effect our request would have had if granted? God loves us, He loves us too dearly to leave us to the guidance of our poor judgements; and when He turns a deaf ear to our entreaties, it is as a tender Father would treat the longings of a child for what would work him harm.

20. *Ordinary Duties.*

What more insignificant than the ordinary daily duties of religious life! Each succeeding hour brings with it some allotted task, yet in the faithful performance of these trifling acts of our everyday life lies the secret of true sanctity. Too often the constant repetition of the same acts, though in themselves they be of the holiest nature, makes us go through them in a mechanical way. We meditate, we assist at holy Mass, more from a sense of duty than from any affection to prayer. Our domestic duties, our hours of labour, of teaching, are faithfully discharged but what motive has animated us in their performance? Have we not worked because we *must,* or unconsciously because the bell has rung, rather than from the motive of pleasing God and doing His will?

21.

A sharp tongue is the only edged tool that grows sharper with use.

22. *One Thing Wanting.*

"One thing is wanting to thee." - S. *Luke* 18, 22. How many souls there are upon whom Jesus looks with love, souls who are very dear to His Sacred Heart, for they have done much and sacrificed much for Him. Yet He asks for more, He wants that last sacrifice, the surrender of that secret clinging to some trifling attachment, that their lives may be a perfect holocaust. How many souls hear this little voice, "One thing is wanting to you that you may be perfect," one generous effort to break away from the almost severed ties of self-love, and yet they heed it not. Liberty, home and family they have given up, the joys and pleasures of this world they have despised, for a life of easy comfort they have embraced the poverty of Christ; but still they cling to some trifling gratification, and heed not the pleadings of the Sacred Heart.

23.

Creation implies too things, nothing and God. Strange combination! yet man thinks much of himself. Let him sound the depths of his origin and he will find nothing.

24.

It seems to me that Jesus is asking from me a life in which I am to make war upon "comfortableness" as far as possible, a life without comfort, even that which is allowed by the rule.
The love of Jesus makes the impossible easy and sweet.

25. *Weariness in Penance.*

I have so completely given you into the keeping of our Blessed Lord that what you tell me does not make me uneasy. Perhaps you have been a little overgenerous and imprudent, and have taxed your strength too much. But even from your present state you may draw much spiritual profit. It will serve to humble you, to show you how utterly dependent you are on God, and to make you trust Him more in the future. I thank Him that you are suffering, for that is sweet to His Heart, and will ease the pain of love in yours. After all you have not yet "resisted unto blood," nor has sheer physical weakness made you faint, as Jesus did.

Still the immolation He wants from you now is the hardest of all the sacrifice of your will to the will of your Superior. Obey her exactly in everything, and till the end of the month lay aside all penance, and "let nature caper!"

26.

Jesus is looking at me as once He did upon blind Bartimeus. "What wilt thou that I do to thee?" - *Luke* 18, 41. Lord, that I may see myself as You see me. Lord, that my eyes may be open to the shortness of life. Lord, that I may understand the value of one degree of merit, and so heap up many.

27. *Never Mind Feelings.*

You seem to be a little upset at not being able to feel more that you really love our Lord. The mere longing desire to do so is a certain proof that love, and much of it, exists in your heart. But you can test your love infallibly and find out how much you have by asking yourself this question: What am I willing to suffer for Him? It is the test of St. Francis de Sales: "Willingness to suffer is a certain proof of love." This question I will answer for you. Though naturally you dread and shrink from pain and humiliation, I am certain there is no humiliation or suffering which you would refuse to accept if God asked you to bear it. That being so, you can say to our Lord with all the confidence of Peter who seemed to doubt his own heart: Lord, Thou knowest that I love Thee with all my heart and soul and strength, for I would gladly lay down my life for Thee.

28. *Illness.*

I was about to commence my letter with the formula: "I am very sorry to hear you are ill," when it struck me that these words were not true. How could you or I be sorry to be the instrument in carrying out the wishes and the will of One we love, and how could I be sorry for what draws you nearer to God's loving Heart sweet pain? All the same I have felt for you these days past, knowing that you must have suffered a good deal.

29.

We must be *intellectually* pious, that is, our piety should rest on the bed-rock of principle, and not on mood, on sentiment, on spiritual con solation.

30.

Agere Contra! Going against self! not in one thing or in two, but in all things where a free choice is left us. These little words contain the life-story of the saints, as they are the weapon that gained the victory which gave them heaven.

31. *We do not Pray Enough.*

You seem lately to have had a bad attack of want of confidence in God and a feeling of despair of ever becoming a saint. Yet, my dear child, it is neither impossible nor hopeless as long as God leaves it in our power to pray. You know these words of Fr. de Ravignan (leaflet enclosed). I never realized how true they were until I began to go about the country and get into touch with souls. I assert fearlessly that if only we all prayed enough and I mean by that a constant, steady, unflagging stream of aspirations, petitions, etc., from the heart there is not one, no matter how imperfect, careless or even sinful, who would not become a saint and a big one. I am perfectly and painfully con-scious that, for my own part, I do not pray a hundredth part of what I should or what God wants. Prayer, then, being the key to sanctity, never tell me again, my dear child, that there is no chance of your becoming a saint. But you certainly never will until you learn to turn every action into a prayer and shake off the old tempter who strangles your efforts to pray.

June

1. *A Transport of Love.*

Jesus is the most loving of lovable friends there never was a friend like Him before, there never can be one to equal Him, because there is only one Jesus in the whole wide world and the vast expanse of Heaven; and that sweet and loving friend, that true lover of the holiest and purest love is *my Jesus,* mine alone and all mine. Every fibre of His divine nature is thrilling with love for me, every beat of His gentle Heart is a throb of intense affection for me, His sacred arms are round me, He draws me to His breast, He bends down with infinite tenderness over me, His child, for He knows I am all His and He is all mine. In His eyes the vast world, the myriads of other souls have all vanished; He has forgotten them all, for that brief moment they do not exist for even the infinite love of God Himself is not enough to pour out on the soul who is clinging so lovingly to Him.

O Jesus, Jesus, Jesus! who would not love You, who would not give their heart's blood for You, if only once they realised the depth and the breadth and the realness of Your burning love? Why not then make every human heart a burning furnace of love for You, so that sin would become an impossibility, sacrifice a pleasure and a joy, virtue the longing of every soul, so that we should live for love, dream of love, breathe Your love, and at last die of a broken heart of love, pierced through and through with the shaft of love, the sweetest gift of God to man.

2. *Wanted: A Chosen Band.*

I think it is evident that, in these days of awful sin and hatred of God, our Blessed Lord wants to gather round Him a legion of chosen souls who will be devoted, heart and soul, to Him and His interests, and upon whom He may always count for help and consolation. Souls who will not ask "How much *must* I do?" but rather "How much *can* I do for His love?" A legion of souls who will give and not count the cost, whose only pain will be that they cannot do more and give more and suffer more for Him who has done so much for them. In a word souls who are not as the rest of men, fools perhaps in the eyes of the world, for their watchword is *sacrifice* and not self-comfort.

Now, my dear child, our divine Saviour seems to have turned His eyes of love upon you and asked you are you willing to join His Body guard; not on account of any merit or good quality on your part, but, as He told B. Margaret Mary, because you are an abyss of unworthiness in His pure eyes. Still, it should make your heart bound with joy to think that He has given you such a loving call; for if only you are faithful to Him and exact in following His inspirations, He will raise you to a height of sanctity you do not dare to dream of now.

3. *"Communia non Communiter."*

I will strive ever to perform each action as perfectly as possible, paying special attention to small duties e.g. saying grace, odd Hail Marys, etc. It seems to me God is asking this particularly from me, and by this means I am to find the chief road to sanctity.

4. *The First Step.*

While making the Holy Hour to-day, the Feast of the Sacred Heart, I felt inspired to make this resolution: Sweet Jesus, as a first step towards my becoming a saint, which You desire so much, I will try to do each duty, each little action, as perfectly and fervently as I possibly can. St. John Berchmans, help me.

5.

As regards the Holy Hour I would urge you personally not to make a practice of staying up every Thursday night. The privation of sleep tells in the end, and you are not too strong; and if you get knocked up, people will say that was the cause and may even get the Hour forbidden. God likes generosity, but we must be prudent and not expect Him to work miracles.

6.

One passage in the little book you sent me struck me very much. "Love grows from love like wheat from wheat." Just as one tiny grain will bring forth an ear filled with many new grains, and each of these, if sown, will bear other ears, so one little act of the love of God is enough to produce in time a very harvest of golden acts.

7. *Dry Adoration.*

Real devotion to the Blessed Sacrament is only to be gained by hard, grinding work of dry adoration before the Hidden God. But such a treasure cannot be purchased at too great a cost, for once obtained, it makes of this life as near an approach to heaven as we can ever hope for.

8. *The Hound of Heaven.*

What you say is indeed true. Jesus has been "hunting" me during these past days, trying to wound my heart with His arrows of love. He has been so gentle, so patient, tender, loving, I do not know at times where to turn, and yet I somehow feel that much of this grace is given me for others, I know it has helped souls and lifted them close to Jesus.

I long to get back to my little room at night, to calm and quiet, and yet I dread it, for He is often so loving there. I feel He is near because I cannot go to Him in the Tabernacle. It is such a helpless feeling to be tossed about as it were on the waves of love, to feel the ardent, burning love of His Heart, to know He asks for love, and then to realise one human heart is so tiny.

Your letter and little meditation have helped me. At times I have smiled at the folly of what you say since I realize how little you know of my real character, and then like a big wave the truth seems to burst on me, that as a fierce fire sweeps away and consumes all obstacles, so the love of God blots out the many faults and failings of my poor life and leaves me free to go to Him.

9.

My denial of Jesus has been baser than that of Peter, for I have refused to listen to His voice calling me back for fifteen years. But Jesus has won my heart in this retreat by His patient look of love. God grant my repentance may in some degree be like St. Peter s. I could indeed weep bitterly for the wasted sinful past in the Society, the time I have squandered, the little good done, and the amount of harm done by my bad example in every house in which I have been. What might I not have done for Jesus! What a saint I might have been now! Dear Jesus, You forgave St. Peter, forgive me also for I *will* serve You now.

10. *The Love of Jesus.*

Lord, You know I love You less than any other, but I long and desire to love You more than all the rest. Take my heart, dear Lord, and hide it in Your own, that so I may only love what You love and desire what You desire. May I find no pleasure in the things of this world, its pleasures and amusement; but may my one delight be in thinking of You, working for You, loving You, and staying in Your sweet presence before the Tabernacle. Why do You want my love, dear Jesus, and why have You left me no rest all these years till I gave You at last my poor heart to love You, and You alone? This cease less pleading for my love fills me with hope and confidence that, sinful as my life has been in the past, You have forgiven and forgotten it all. Thanks a million times, dearest Jesus, for all Your goodness. I *will* love and serve You now till death.

11.

The Gospel says: "In the daytime He was teaching in the Temple." - S. *Luke*, 21, 37. How often, and for how long, am I in the chapel? Is the chapel the place where people know I am to be found? What a difference it would make in my visits, if only I *realised* the real corporal presence of Jesus in the Tabernacle. This is a grace I must earnestly ask for.

12. *The Third Degree of Humility.*

1. - *Accepto.* I will receive with joy all unpleasant things which I must bear: (*a*) pain, sickness, heat, cold, food; (*b*) house, employment, rules, customs; (*c*) trials of religious life, companions; (*d*) reprimands, humiliations; (*e*) anything which is a cross.
2. - *Volo et desidero.* I will wish and desire that these things may happen to me, that so I may resemble my Jesus more.

3. - Eligo. With all my might I will strive every day *agere contra in omnibus:* (*a*) against my faults; (*b*) against my own will; (*c*) against my ease and comfort; (*d*) against the desires of the body; (*e*) against my habit and inclination of performing my duties negligently and without fervour.

13. *The Moment of Benediction.*

The priest turns and raises aloft the Sacred Host. In loving adoration, in reverent awe, the invisible angels fall prostrate. The bell tinkles softly, fragrant clouds of sweet-smelling incense ascend on high, and in the remotest corner of the vast church every head is bowed in adoration. It is a solemn moment, a moment when the silent streams of grace pour down upon our souls. God's hands are lifted up to bless us; His sacred face is turned upon us, and He waits oh! so eagerly for us to ask some favour that He may win our hearts by His generosity. Let us ask, then, confidently and show our trust in God's great goodness by the boldness of our requests.

14. *Following My Leader.*

I feel that I could go through fire and water to serve such a man as Napoleon, that no sacrifice he could ask would be too hard. What would the army think of me if Napoleon said, "I want you to do so and so," and I replied, "But, your Majesty, I am very sensitive to cold, I want to have a sleep in the afternoon, to rest when I am tired, and I really could not do without plenty of good things to eat!" would I not deserve to have my uniform torn from me and be driven from the army, not even allowed to serve in the ranks? How do I serve Jesus my King? What kind of service? generous or making conditions? in easy things but not in hard ones? What have I done for Jesus? What am I doing for Jesus? What shall I do for Jesus?

15.

One thing I ask of you, dear child: Don't be a saint by halves, but give Him all He asks and always.

16. *Human Respect.*

One of the obstacles to my leading a fervent life is the thought of what others may think. I would often wish to do some act of mortification, but I am prevented because I know others will see it. Again, I desire to keep certain rules which I have broken (*e.g.* Latin conversation), but a false shame, a fear of what others may say, stops me. I know this is a foolish, mean and small spirit; but it is alas! too true in my case. I must pray to overcome it and make some generous acts against this false shame and pride.

17. *Generosity.*

I feel also a great longing to love Jesus very, very much, to draw very close to His Sacred Heart, and to be ever united to Him, always thinking of Him and praying. I long ardently to do something now to make up for my neglect in the past to give myself heart and soul to the service of God, to toil for Him, to wear myself out for Him. I wish to be able never to seek rest or amusement outside of what obedience imposes, so that every moment may be spent for Jesus. I have not a moment to lose, I cannot afford to refuse Him a single sacrifice if I wish to do anything for Jesus and become a saint before I die. If I go to the Congo, I certainly shall not live long. In any case can I promise myself even one day more? I must try to look upon this day as my last on earth and do all I can and suffer all I can for these few hours. It is not a question of keeping up full steam for years, but only for to-day.

If I am faithful to the resolution of "doing all things perfectly," I shall effectually cut away the numerous faults in all my actions. By working hard at the Third Degree I shall best correct those things to which my attention has been drawn. I know all this is going to cost me much, that I shall have a fierce battle to fight with the devil and myself. But I begin with great hope and confidence, for since Jesus has inspired me to make these resolutions and urged me on till I did so, His grace will not be wanting to aid me at every step.

In the name of God, then, I enter upon the Narrow Path which leads to sanctity, walking bravely on in imitation of my Jesus who is by my side carrying His cross. To imitate Him and make my life resemble His in some small degree, will be my life's work, that so I may be worthy to die for Him.

18. *All for Jesus.*

A great desire to know our Lord better, His attractive character, His personal love for me, the resolve to read the life of Christ and study the Gospels.

I feel also a longing to love Jesus passionately, to try my very best to please Him, and to do all I think will please Him. I see nothing will be dearer to Him than my sanctification, chiefly attained by the perfection with which I perform even the smallest action. "All for love of Jesus."

The reason, said Fr. Petit, why we find life so hard, mortification difficult, and why we are inclined to avoid all that we dislike, is because we have *no real love for Jesus.*

19. *Immolation.*

As regards the Act of Immolation *(See 17th of March)* I give you full permission to make it. But do not complain to our dear Lord if He takes you at your word and makes you His victim. You need not fear whatever He may send you to bear, since His grace will come with it; but you should always try to keep in mind your offering, living up to the spirit of it. Hence endeavour to see the hand of God in everything that happens to you now; *e.g.* if you rise in the morning with a head ache, thank Him for sending it, since a victim is one who must be immolated and crucified. Again, look upon all humiliations and crosses, failure and disappointment in your work, in a word, everything that is hard, as His seal upon your offering, and rouse yourself to bear all cheerfully and lovingly, remembering that you are to be His "suffering love."

20. *Love, Prayer, Sacrifice.*

I have long had the feeling that, since the world is growing so rapidly worse and worse and God has lost His hold, as it were, upon the hearts of men, He is looking all the more earnestly and anxiously for big things from those who are faithful to Him still. He cannot, perhaps, gather a large army round His standard, but He wants every one in it to be a *hero,* absolutely and lovingly devoted to Him. If only we could get inside that magic circle of generous souls, I believe there is no grace He would not give us to help on the work He has so much at heart, our personal sanctification. Every day you live means an infallible growth in holiness which may be multiplied a thousand times by a little generosity. When you get the chance hammer into the "Little Flowers" around you that holiness means three things: - Love, Prayer, Sacrifice.

21. *God's Hand.*

"No evil shall come upon you." - *Jerem.* 23. 17, It is a consoling thought that God watches over us with unceasing care; that no matter where we may be alone in our humble cell or passing through the crowded streets of the feverish panting city the hand of God is over us and sheltering us from a thousand unknown dangers, guiding us safely along the path of life. Wicked men may plot evil things against us, all the hellish horde may rage in fury round us, but harm us they cannot without His consent who directs all things for His own wise ends. Poverty may be our lot, sickness may lay its heavy hand upon us, and misfortunes thickly strew our path. But welcome be they all! They are precious gifts from the hand of a loving Saviour.

22. *Worrying about Faults.*

I fear you are allowing the devil to score off you by getting so much upset over these bother some, but harmless, temptations. You must let our Lord sanctify you in His own way. Were we to pick our own trials and modes of sanctification, we should soon make a mess of things. The net result of your temptations is a deeper humility, a sense of your own weakness and wretchedness, and is not this all gain? "My brethren, count it all joy, when you shall fall into divers temptations," says St. James (1. 2). All I ask you to do is to try to crush down the first movements of temptation, which perhaps can best be done by praying that others may be more favoured or esteemed than you. There is a danger you may not suspect in thinking and grieving too much over temptation and faults. First of all there is oftentimes a secret pride hidden in our grief and anger with ourselves for not being as perfect as we thought, or as others thought. Then this worrying over what cannot well be avoided distracts the soul from God. After all, what God wants from you, my child, is love, and nothing should distract you from the grand work of love-giving. Hence when you fail, treat our Blessed Lord like a loving little child, tell Him you are sorry, kiss His feet as a token of your regret, and then forget all about your naughtiness.

23.

In the matter of suffering I think you are inclined to confound the act of the will with feeling. You do not really "draw back" when suffering comes, since you have the will to bear all things for the love of Jesus; but nature shrinks from pain and at times makes our "will to suffer" give way.

24.

Do nothing without consulting Him in the Tabernacle. But then act fearlessly, if you see it is for His honour and glory, never minding what others may think or say. Above all, "cast your care upon the Lord and He shall sustain you." - *Psalm* 54. 23. Peace and calm in your soul, prayer ever on your lips, and a big love in your heart for Him and His interests, will carry you very far.

25.

No sound breaks the holy silence of the dim-lit chapel. All is hushed and mute. Faintly the pale light of the ruby lamp throws its soft beams on the marble altar, as if to envelop the Prisoner of Love with its rays and make up for the cold ness of men's hearts.

26. *"Let Him Act."*

May our dear Lord help you to bear the cross His love has sent you. Try to keep this one thought before you all through your trial: This is God's doing. Hence do not indulge in useless regrets about want of care, etc. Even if there was negligence, God permitted it to give you this golden chance of being brave and generous under the cross. What has happened will bring you much grace and even happiness, if you take it in the right way. "Let Him act," must be your motto. Jesus will bring all things right in the end. The more I get to know God, the more inclined I feel to let Him work out things in His own way and time, and to go on peacefully not troubling about anything. This cross is a sign of God's love for you, and the surest way of increasing your love for Him. Though you indeed try to take courageously the crosses God sends you, still there seems to be a want of that complete submission to God's wishes that He looks for and longs for in every detail of your life. Endeavour still more to give Him the desire of His Heart.

27.

"Come in before His presence with exceeding great joy." - *Psalm* 99, 2. Yes, come before Jesus in the Blessed Eucharist with a joyous heart, for He, the bounteous giver of all good gifts, will fill it with His grace. Make haste and tarry not. He waits for your coming, as the tender mother yearns for the absent child she loves so dearly, that He may load you with His heavenly treasures and send you away with "joy exceeding great."

28.

I do not think your "false humility" is pleasing to God, though I do not suggest for a moment that you are putting it on. Drop self and all thought of reparation out of your life, and work now only for Him and the salvation of souls. If an aspiration, on the authority of the B. Cure d Ars, often saved a soul, what must you not do each day you suffer so bravely! This thought certainly will help you and make the pain almost nothing, and will add to its merit, since the motive for bearing it will be all the higher.

29. *Christ's Mercy.*

"Let the mercies of the Lord give glory to Him." Psalm 106, 21. Jesus during His mortal life practised many virtues; but none is more conspicuous, none appeals more strongly to us, than His infinite mercy, His tender forgiveness of all injuries. A vile sinner is brought before Him, her very mien proclaims her crime. "Have none condemned thee? Neither shall I. Go, sin no more." Magdalen, the bye-word of the city, Magdalen whose name was sin and shame, seeks His forgiveness and finds His mercy. Peter, the favoured one, denies his Master and turns his back on Him who loved him so; and Peter's heart is won, even in his sin, by one loving look of mercy and compassion from the Saviour whose mercy is without end.

30.

Devotion to the Sacred Heart cannot exist without self-denial, the flames and thorns around that Heart, the cross that crowns It, point to a love of and call for suffering.

July

1. *The Devil's "Pet Walking-Stick."*

There is one fault in religious which should not be forgiven either in this world or in the world to come, and that is *discouragement;* for it means we are playing the devil's game for him his pet walking-stick, someone has called it. Thank God, we have not to judge ourselves, for, as St. Ignatius wisely remarks, no one is a judge in his own case. Let me judge you, my child, as I honestly think God judges you. My verdict must be that you have grown immensely in holiness during the past few years. To begin with, every particle of merit and there must be millions of them since you first entered religion is waiting for you in heaven, for no amount of infidelity or venial sin can ever diminish that by one iota. Then, in spite of your sufferings and weak health, you have worked on and struggled on from day to day a life which must have pleased God immensely. Don't lose heart, my dear child, the darkness you feel is not a sign of God's displeasure, for every saint has gone through it. You are "minting money" every instant you live, you are helping to save soul after soul each hour you suffer. So you should say with St. Paul, (2 *Cor.* 7. 4) "I exceedingly abound with joy in all our tribulation."

2. *Past Confessions.*

I hope by the time you receive this you will have realised how foolish it is of you to bother about anything no matter what it may be in your past confessions. Generously make the sacrifice of never thinking or speaking of them again. You may do so with an easy conscience when you act under obedience. God wants to have your soul in a state of perfect peace and calm, for only then will He be able to fill it with His love and dwell there undisturbed.

3. *An Act of the Love of God.*

Have you ever reflected on the power of an act of the love of God, when inspired by grace and made with faith? Let us recall to mind the simple words of which it is composed:

My God, I love You with my whole heart, with my whole soul, with all my strength, and above all things; because You are good, infinitely good.

Try to pronounce each word so slowly that it may sink into your heart.

Do you not feel that in making this act, you give your whole life to God, you give more than if you gave your riches, your time, your strength? Or rather that this act of love transports you out of yourself and gives to God your whole being and all that you possess?

I defy you, guilty, desolate, despairing soul, soul overwhelmed by terror, dread, and the fear of damnation I defy you to go before a crucifix or before the holy Tabernacle and say to Jesus, dwelling the more on the words the harder you find it to say them, "My God, I love You with my whole heart...because You are infinitely good," and not feel that Jesus is moved by your words, and not hear Jesus reply, "And I too love you." Reason not on this. Try it. Could you believe of Jesus Christ that He does not know how to love or that His Heart is less generous than yours?

O Jesus! how can I find words to express the love with which your Sacred Heart responds to a word of tenderness from a poor child of earth! That Heart so tender, so sensitive, so loving!

There is a little sentence of Fr. Faber's which, to minds less spiritual, sounds strange: "God tries to win our affections, to force us to love Him, that in return He may not only love us, for that He does already, but that He may make us feel that He loves us."

4. *The Power of an Act of Love.*

To make an act of love requires but a few seconds. We can make these acts at any hour, we can multiply them, and how wonderful is their effect!

We delight the Heart of Jesus and cause Him to shed more abundant graces on the world. The Blessed Virgin rejoices, her love for us increases, and she thanks us for them. Our guardian angel listens with emotion and comes closer to us as if to make us feel that we have done well. The angels regard us with ineffable tenderness and joy. The power of the demons is lessened and for a moment their temptations cease. The choirs of the Blessed in Heaven redouble their canticles of joy.

Who would not during the day multiply acts of love?

You who are reading this, pause a minute and say, "My God, I love You! My God, I love You!"

Grant us, O Lord, the twofold spirit of devotion to Your service and of holy fear, tempered and mastered by confidence and love.

5. *Abandonment.*

I would like you to know what I think Jesus wants from you. He would like you to place yourself in His hands entirely, giving Him full permission to do what He likes with you. Thus you will accept lovingly crosses, trials, joys and sickness, which you will try to take from His loving hands as a proof of love. Don't ask for suffering, but open your arms wide if it comes. Abandon yourself to Him to do as He pleases. Hence the keynote of your life must be sacrifice. For a victim that is not sacrificed is not a victim.

6. *Peace the Measure of Mortification.*

The mortification good for you may be measured by your peace of mind. If you find your soul troubled by the penance you practise, or feel urged to practise, you should suspect the spirit that is leading you. Give all you can, but let it be the "cheerful giver," whom God loves. When the sacrifice is costing you too much and ruffles the spirit, go a little slower and all will be well.

7. *"Ammunition" for the Missions.*

I cannot tell you how grateful I am for your offering of Masses and prayers. It is what I call my "ammunition" for the missions, which will mean the capture of many a poor sinner. If only you knew what a help and encouragement it is, I think you would be well rewarded, and perhaps more anxious to aid the "toilers in the vine yard," who depend on prayer to bless their work and make it fruitful.

8. *Suffer Willingly.*

God wants you to suffer willingly. Many rebel and fight against what God gives them; many more take their cross in a resigned "can't be helped" spirit; but very few look upon these things as real blessings and kiss the Hand that strikes them.

9.

During the last few days the thought has come home to me that the truest title to address our divine Lord by is "Poor Jesus." He is rich in all things except the one He really cares about the love of loving hearts.

10. *Love of Jesus.*

I cannot deny that I love Jesus, love Him passionately, love Him with every fibre of my heart. He knows it, too, since He has asked me to do many things for Him which have cost me more than I should like to say, yet which with His grace were sweet and easy in a sense. He knows that my longing, at least, even if the strength and courage are wanting, is to do and suffer much more for Him, and that were He to-morrow to ask for the sacrifice of every living friend, I would not refuse Him. Yet with all that, with the intense longing to make Him known and loved, I have never yet been able to speak of Him to others as I want to.

11. *Holiness is not in a Vocabulary.*

I would strongly advise you not to read books treating of the mystical life unless you can get a good guide. You might be imagining yourself in a certain state when you are a thousand miles away from it. ...Go on quietly, loving God and seeking to please Him, without trying to find out in what exact state of perfection your soul is.

12. *The Secret Apostolate.*

Yon are treading in the right path, the path our divine Lord wants you to walk in, that of humiliation and suffering. It seems to me that these are the two things dearest to His Heart and that when He finds a soul willing to take up this secret apostleship, His love and affection for that soul, no matter how unworthy in other respects, seems to have no bounds. It was this willing ness in you, my child, to be humbled and trodden under the feet of all, which first drew down His eyes of mercy. And now that you have offered yourself as His Victim to be consumed in the furnace of suffering should He so wish it, there is no grace He will not bestow on you. But remember the devil will spoil the work if he can and by every means in his power turn you from your life of immolation. However I know you are brave and loving, which will carry you over many a difficulty. *Sursum corda.* Often look upwards towards the reward, the price of victory great sanctity and a multitude of souls given back to the arms of Jesus.

13. *Another Day is gone.*

The soft chimes of the angelus bell mark the fall of evening. Another day is gone. Another precious day, our measurement of God's most precious gift, time, has passed away and is swallowed up in the vast gulf of the irrevocable past. Another day has past! Another stage of our journey towards our final end is traversed. Nearer still than yesterday to that solemn moment of our lives, its end; nearer still to heaven with its joys unknown, untasted; nearer still to Him for Whom we labour now and strive to serve. How many more days are left? Too few alas! for all we have to do, but not so few that we cannot heap them high with noble deeds and victories bravely won.

14. *How to acquire close Union.*

The object of my life to be close union with and intense love of God. To acquire this I will (*a*) fly from the shadow of sin, never deliberately break a rule, custom or regulation; (*b*) do each little action purely for the love of Jesus, with exquisite exactness, fervour and devotedness; (*c*) beg constantly and earnestly for a great increase of love.

15. *Inner Peace and Union.*

Now, my child, that you are working on the right lines towards holiness, that is, aiming at a life of constant close union with our Lord, you must expect the devil's attacks. His aim will be to destroy your *peace of soul,* without which there can be no life of union.

Work away at the life of union, but union remember with God *within* you, not outside; so many go wrong on this point. Do not give up prayer on any account, no matter how dry or "rotten" you feel; every moment, especially before Him in the Tabernacle, is a certain, positive gain; the effect will be there though you may not feel it. If you feel drawn "to rest in God," to let yourself sink down as it were into Him, do so without bothering to say anything. I think the best of all prayers is just to kneel quietly and let Jesus pour Himself into your soul.

16. *God works through us.*

I have come back from the missions with feelings of joy and gratitude, for these last three missions have been blessed in a wonderful way. God seems to take a special delight in seconding my efforts, just because I have hurt Him so much in the past and have been so really ungrateful. It is one of the big humiliations of my life and makes me thoroughly ashamed of myself that our Blessed Lord for His own wise ends conceals my shortcomings from others and allows me to do a little good. But He does not hide the wretched state of my soul from myself. I am not speaking in a false humble strain, but serious truth. If you, or anyone else, could only see the way I have acted towards Jesus all my life, you would turn away from me in disgust.

I have had much consolation in my work recently. The last mission was the hardest I have given, yet it seems to have been singularly blessed. All this love and goodness on the part of Jesus only fills me with a deep sorrow that I can do so little for Him. I am getting afraid of Him, just because He is so generous to me and blesses all I do. I feel ashamed when people praise me for my work, the sort of shame a piano might feel if someone complimented it on the beautiful melody that came from its keys. I am realizing more and more that all success is entirely God's work, and that self does not count at all. I have this strange feeling that when I get to heaven I shall have little merit for anything I have done for God's glory, since all has been the work of His Hands.

17.

The reformation of one's life must be the work of every day. I should take each rule and duty, think how Jesus acted, or would have done, and contrast my conduct with His.

18.

I was greatly struck and helped yesterday by these words of the "Imitation": *Fili, sine me tecum agere quod volo, ego scio quid expediat tibi.* [1] They gave me courage to place myself without reserve in God's hands. How happy I feel now that I have done so and made my sacrifice.

19. *No Cowardice.*

Believe me, I feel intensely for you, my child, for I know what you have suffered in the past and how violent the attacks of the tempter have been. But this very thing ought to be a big joy to you, since it shows how much the evil one fears what you are going to do for our Blessed Lord and poor perishing souls. If you were not a dangerous "enemy," he would leave you alone, but he cannot help showing his hand. That being so, you can easily see how foolish it would be to yield to him now after so many heroic victories. Besides, I promise you this, that if you fight the temptations for a little while, great peace will soon come. Your only mistake has been to show the "white feather" even a little. Be brave and generous, my child, for the sake of our dear Lord, who loves you so much, as you know so well. If you have given in a little, don't lose a moment, but start away again. I shall pray for you, but you must pray for yourself.

20. *So few really generous Souls.*

Life is only a day quickly passed and gone, but the merit of it, the glory given to God, will remain for ever. Give Him all you can generously and lovingly, do not let one little sacrifice escape you, they are dear to Him because He finds so few really generous souls who think only of Him and never of themselves.

21.

"I will give thee hidden treasures." *Isaiah* 45. 3. Jesus has treasures which He hides from those who love Him not and do not seek Him. To His favoured ones, His faithful servants, He opens wide the storehouse where they lie and pours His graces forth unmeasured. He is a hidden God. He dwells not with the proud and haughty. He lingers not amid the tumult of the world.

22. *S. Mary Magdalen.*

Jesus allowed her to wash His feet but knew well what those eyes had looked on. He allowed her lips to kiss His feet knowing what sinful words had fallen from them. He did not shrink from the touch of hands which had served Satan so long. He even welcomed the love of a heart so long filled with unholy desires. Mary, penitent as she is, could not fully know the depth of her guilt, she had forgotten many sins; but Jesus saw all....

In those few moments Mary had learnt a precious lesson: that peace, contentment, holiness are to be found at the feet of Jesus and there alone, that the delights of contemplation far outweighs the empty joys which the world offers.

23. *Advice on Penance.*

I do not want, in fact I forbid you, to be imprudent in the matter of corporal penances. But, my dear child, if you let a whole fortnight go by without any self-inflicted pain, can you honestly look Jesus in the face and say, "I am like to Him."?

To another Correspondent.

I want you to give up *all* corporal penance and to take for your particular examen "self-denial in little things." Make ten acts for each examen, and the more trivial they are the better, so you will do twenty a day.

24. *A Heart-Hermitage.*

A quiet hidden life is not possible for you in one way, and yet perfectly so in another by building a solitude in your heart where you can ever live alone with Jesus, letting the noise and worry of life, cares and anxieties of the world, pass over your head, like a storm which will never ruffle the peace of your soul. You will enjoy perfect calm and peace of soul, the requisite condition for a life of union, by keeping Jesus ever with you as a Friend, and remembering that everything happens by His permission and is in fact His work. Let this principle soak in and it will make you a saint. Apply it to every detail of your life, and you will not be far from what you seek; in fact humiliations, slights, annoyances, worries will all disappear, since it is not X, but Jesus, who is trying you in this way.

25. *S. James.*

You ask how to pray well. The answer is, Pray often, in season and out of season, against yourself, in spite of yourself. There is no other way. What a man of prayer St. James, the Apostle (his feast is to-day) must have been since his knees became like those of a camel! When shall we religious realize the power for good that prayer, constant, unflagging prayer, puts into our hands? Were you convinced of this, you would not "envy me my spiritual work." Because if you liked, you could do more than any priest who is not a man of prayer, though you might not have the satisfaction of seeing the result in this world. Did it ever strike you that when our Lord pointed out the "fields white for the harvest," He did not urge His Apostle to go and reap it, but *to pray*?

26. *Confession.*

As regards having natural motives for Confession this would of course make it invalid but only if one were absolutely to exclude all super natural motives, which is practically impossible. Besides, natural motives may exist provided the supernatural is there also. Thus the desire to unburden one's mind and chat about things might be only a natural motive, but the desire to get rid of the sin supplies the supernatural part. I am shocked to think you have missed even one absolution. I, too, used long ago to hate Confession, for no reason whatever, till as a priest I began to realize the fact that it is the biggest help and quickest means to holiness, since a Sacrament pours grace into the soul. Don't examine your conscience! If there is a big fault it will stand out and show itself; if not, any sin will do for absolution; there is no fear of bad or careless confessions. Go every day if you can.

God bless you, my dear child. Keep on steadily with great confidence and patience with your self; do not look too much for results from your efforts to be a saint, the work is being done silently but surely.

27. *A Vocation.*

I assure you that you have my entire sympathy as well as my prayers in the trial you are going through. There are few things more painful than to long to know the Will of God and not be able to see it, though it may be quite clear to others. From all that has passed between us I have no doubt that you have a religious vocation. Look at it in this way. Our Lord makes known His willingness to receive anyone into religion by giving them the necessary qualifications and the wish to do this work there. If I have these qualifications "aptitude," it is called and this wish, all I need is the *will* to take the step. What you have to do is to pray for strength to be brave. Then go ahead, trust in the Sacred Heart, and you will never regret it.

28. *Begin Again.*

I am sorry to see you are hoisting the devil's flag of discouragement. It is a precious lesson of the spiritual world that there must be ups and downs even with the most earnest efforts and in the holiest lives. "Begin again" is the motto of success in the path of holiness. Remember, too, that faults and falls rightly used help to teach us our weakness and to make us humble, and so are really a stepping-stone to greater sanctity.

29.

The famous Mother Agnes who converted M. Olier, the saviour of the priests of France, once wrote to him: "I love your soul so much I pray our

Lord every day to send you nothing but crosses and afflictions." If this is not my prayer, at least it is my wish for you too, and so, though I feel for you in your suffering, which I know must have been intense, still I am glad of this mark of Jesus love for His spouse and victim.

30.

Every day sanctifying grace is increasing in your soul in spite of faults and failings, therefore every day you are more pleasing to God even though you pain Him by infidelities. You can say each day: "I am holier than I was yesterday."

31.

Keep in God's presence going through the house and try to grasp then any lights you may have got in prayer.

[1] "My child, let Me do with you what I will; I know what is good for you." - *Imitation of Christ* iii. 17, 1. A favourite quotation of Fr. Doyle's.

August

1. *Four Dangers to be Feared after a Retreat.*

1. Dissipation: There, it is over; amuse your self. **2.** Toning Down: Too much, too many, too hard, too often, too etc. **3.** Putting Off: Wait a little, rest yourself, take your time. **4.** Cowardice: You'll never do it; you re no good; it will be the same old story.

And Four Remedies.

1. Presence of God: No, it is not over, it is only just begun. **2.** Exactness: No such thing; I'll do all I have resolved; nothing too much for God. **3.** Promptitude: No, at once; here goes; I may die to-day. **4.** Determination: We'll see; I am no good, but Someone good and powerful is with me.

2. *Broken Resolutions.*

I hope every single one of you will have broken every resolution you made in the retreat before the end of the week, and if not then, at least in a fortnight. It will do you good and humble you provided you get up and begin again and do not flop down and lie there on the broad of your back, saying "It's no use, It's all over." Not a bit of it, It's not all over, It's only beginning. So up with you and start again. Remember each time you fall that you are not back where you were before but are starting again from where you fell.

3. *Keep your Will Firm.*

St. Vincent de Paul used to say: "One of the most certain marks that God has great designs upon a soul is when He sends desolation upon desolation, suffering upon suffering." Do you doubt for a moment that God has not great designs upon your soul? The clear and consoling proof is in the terrible trial you are going through. Do not let the assaults of the enemy disturb you. He is showing his hand by this last storm and his fierce fury that you did not yield in the direction that he wanted. Treat his suggestions with silent contempt, simply lifting your heart to God now and again, but above all not trying to *drive* these thoughts away, nor being fearful of giving any consent even though you may seem to do so under the violence of the attack. Keep your will firm, and do not trouble about feelings.

4. *Desires.*

I can well understand the pain of longing to love Him intensely and at the same time being powerless to prove that love. But, my child, you have a powerful weapon in your hand desires. Desires please Him immensely. Often repeat your desire to love.

5.

Your ardent desire to love God is the best proof of a real love for Him. But are we not all very much to blame for not growing faster in this love, since we have the certain means in our hands? Ten little acts a day "My God, I love You" mean ten new degrees of love in our hearts. So it is only a question of *persevering work* to reach a big real love for Him. Every action can be made into an act of love which will infallibly increase our store each day.

6. *Childlikeness.*

The more lowly, humble and childlike you are, the more will you win the love and affection of Jesus. I wonder that we do not think more on His clear teaching about sanctity: Unless you become as a child, you will never be a saint.

7. *Familiar Love.*

The wretched spirit of Jansenism has driven our dear Lord from His rightful place in our heart. He longs for love and familiar love, so give Him both I need not say when others do not see you. ... I know a holy soul who never leaves the chapel without kissing the Tabernacle door and walking backward, kissing her hand to the Prisoner of Love.

8. *Pain is the Price of Love.*

You must bear in mind that, if God has marked you out for very great graces and possibly a holiness of which you do not even dream, you must be ready to suffer; and the more of this comes to you, especially sufferings of soul, the happier it ought to make you....Love of God is holiness, but the price of love is *pain*. Round the treasure-house of His love, God has set a thorny hedge; those who would force their way through must not shrink when they feel the sharpness of the thorns piercing their very soul. But alas! how many after a step or two turn sadly back in fear, and so never reach the side of Jesus.

9. *God's Instruments.*

My success here has far surpassed anything I looked for. But it is, of course, the work of God's grace. I do not think I could possibly find food for vainglory in anything I have done, no more than an organ-grinder prides himself on the beautiful music he produces by turning a handle. God knows I only wish and seek His greater glory, and to make others love Him, if I cannot love Him myself. All along I felt it was all His doing, and that I was just a mere instrument in His hands, and a wretched one at that. All through I had the feeling that I was like an old bucket full of holes, which broke the poor Lord's Heart as He tried to carry His precious grace into the hearts of His children.

I think Jesus was pleased with our work here. He certainly showed it on Sunday when I asked Him to give me in honour of His Blessed Mother all the souls I intended to visit that day. They all gave in to His grace, including several who had not been to the sacraments for very many years. People say it is hard to love God. I only wish they could realize how much He loves them and wishes their salvation and happiness.

10. *What we give is not lost.*

Second pilgrimage to Amettes from Locre. During the journey I felt our Lord wanted to give me some message through St. Benedict Joseph Labre. No light came while praying in the Church or in the house; but when I went up to his little room and knelt down a voice seemed to whisper "Read what is written on the wall." I saw these words: *Dieu m' appele á la me austère; il faut que je me prèpare pour suivre les voies de Dieu.* [1] With these words came a sudden light to see how much one gains by every act of sacrifice, that what we give is not lost; but the enjoyment (increased a thousand fold) is only postponed. This filled me with extraordinary consolation which lasted all day.

11.

We have a strict right to the love of God, because our vocation is to follow Him; we cannot do this unless we love Him. Jesus will assuredly give me a sensible love of Him, if I only *ask*. I must ask, seek, and knock daily and hourly.

12.

"What is it to thee? Follow thou Me." - S. *John* 21. 22. This thought came to me: I am not to take the lives of others in the house as the standard of my own, what may be lawful for them is not for me; their life is most pleasing to God, such a life for me would not be so; God wants something higher, nobler, more generous from me, and for this will offer me special graces.

13. *Much without being Singular.*

It is easy for me to test my love for Jesus. Do I love what He loved and came down from heaven to find suffering, humiliation, contempt, want of all things, inconveniences, hunger, weariness, cold? The more I seek for and embrace these things, the nearer am I drawing to Jesus and the deeper is my love for Him. While praying for light to know what God wants from me in the matter of mortifying my appetite, a voice seemed to say: "There are other things besides food in which you can be generous with Me, other *hard things* which I want you to do." I thought of all the secret self-denial contained in constant hard work, not giving up when a bit tired, not yielding to desire for sleep, not running off to bed if a bit unwell, bearing little sufferings without relief, cold and heat without complaint, and, above all, the constant never-ending mortification to do each action *perfectly.* This light has given me a good deal of consolation, for I see I can do much for Jesus that is hard without being singular or departing from common life.

14. *Like Wax in His Hands.*

We do not mind what God does with us so long as it more or less fits in with our own wishes; but when His will clashes with ours, we begin to see the difficulty of the prayer, "Not my will but Thine be done." All the same I think we can never expect really to please God till we become like wax in His hands, so that He will never have to hesitate before sending a cross or trial no matter how hard.

15.

I read through your diary of little victories with intense joy, until I came to the entry, "actually felt glad at receiving a snub to-day," when I felt my cup of happiness was full.... This is what I have been longing for. ... To yearn for, to seek and delight in the hard thing, is not only the road to heroic sanctity, but means a life of wonderful interior joy.

16.

One big fault I note in you discouragement. That must come out of your life at once, my child. Use your faults as "stepping-stones to better things." Don't bemoan your faults and falls, but quietly take it cut of yourself for having given in to nature, and then with a smiling face begin again. Try every day to get a little closer to Jesus.

17. *Holiness is within our reach.*

How many deceive themselves in thinking sanctity consists in the holy follies of the saints! How many look upon holiness as something beyond their reach or capability, and think that it is to be found only in the performance of extraordinary actions. Satisfied that they have not the strength for great austerities, the time for much prayer, or the courage for painful humiliations, they silence their conscience with the thought that great sanctity is not for them, that they have not been called to be saints. With their eyes fixed on the heroic deeds of the few, they miss the daily little sacrifices God asks them to make; and while waiting for something great to prove their love, they lose the countless little opportunities of sanctification each day bears with it in its bosom.

18. *Time.*

What would the damned not give for one moment of the time which we think so little of! If one of these unhappy souls could return again on earth and live again its ill-spent life, how differently it would look upon those things which before it despised? How eagerly it would gather up the fleeting moments that not one even might be lost, but each might bear its burden of mint into eternity. Would it have need, think you, of seeking useless amusements to pass the time? Would its days and years be swallowed up in the vain pursuit of useless trifles, its precious life squandered far from God in the evil haunts of sin? One moment of time for sorrow and repentance would turn the pit of hell into a paradise of delight.

19. *Getting Good out of our Faults.*

In spite of all our efforts, we fall into faults from time to time. God permits this for two reasons: (1) to keep the soul humble and to make it realise its utter powerlessness when left alone without His fostering hand, and (2) because the act of sorrow after the fault not only washes it completely away, but immensely increases our merit, and being an act of humility bringing us really heartbroken to His feet, delights Him beyond measure.

20. *Love the Hard Thing.*

All these trials, snubs, unpleasantnesses, etc., do not come to you by chance, they are precious jewels from the hand of God, and, if you could only bring yourself to look upon them in the right light, would make you a really big saint. Here is how you are to do it. Do you remember a story told of a certain saint who searched the whole city to find the most troublesome, cranky, sick woman in it and then took her into her house and lavished every care upon the wretched creature, who repaid her with curses and in gratitude? The saint bore it all without a murmur and even with joy, because this ill-treatment was the very thing she was in search of, and could she have found a more cross-grained old hag she would have exchanged her with pleasure. Have you learned your lesson? Try and love the "hard thing," wish for it, ask for it provided that God wishes to send it to you, and then when it comes in the shape of an unjust, stinging word, force yourself to say (dryly), "Thank God, now I am holier."

21. *Keep Smiling.*

Keep smiling. It is a grand thing to cultivate a smile. Keep the corners of your mouth up, especially if you are in for an attack of the dumps. There are three Ds to be avoided the Devil, the Doctor, and the Dumps. The Devil, we all know, is bad enough; the Doctor is very little better; and the Dumps are the Devil himself! So I repeat, keep smiling, it is the very best remedy for gloom. The devil loves nothing better than a gloomy soul; it is his plaything.

Smile a while, and while you smile another smiles, and soon there's miles and miles of smiles, and life's worthwhile because you smile.

22. *Without Reserve.*

How many wish to belong entirely to Jesus without reserve or restriction? Most want to serve two masters, to be under two standards. A union of worldliness and devotion; a perpetual succession of sins and repentance; something given to grace, more to nature; fervour and tepidity by turns. Such is the state of many religious. Obligations are whittled down; rules are interpreted laxly; all kinds of excuses are invented for self-indulgence health, greater glory of God in the end, etc. No service is so hard as the half-and-half; what is given to God costs more; His yoke is heavy; the cross is dragged, not cheerfully carried; the thought of what is refused to grace causes remorse and sadness; there is no pleasure from the world and little from the service of Christ.

23.

Look upon the grace God gives you as a talent you must work with and increase. The Master in the Gospel gave his profitable servants twice as many talents. In like manner will God double your grace if you make good use of it. He will give you "grace for grace." - *John* 1. 16.

24.

My dear child, as I have a few spare moments before we set out at 10 p.m. for the firing line, I must send you some words of encouragement.

What has happened, is God's happening. He will bring all things out smoothly and pleasantly in the end. Trust Him. You must try to be patient and wait for God to arrange things in His own way. And His ways are not our ways, remember. Very slow ways, they seem at times! The mills of God grind slowly, but they surely grind!

I am not afraid of your going to X. Its very hardness and disadvantages should attract you all the more since you have learnt that there is no joy like suffering for Jesus. Some saint was asked did he mind going to a certain unpleasant house. "Is Jesus there in the Tabernacle?" he asked. "If so, everything else is of little con sequence." There is much in that, my child, is there not?

God bless you. Now for a night of mud!

25.

I am truly glad you are looking to the perfection of your daily actions; it is the simplest, yet perhaps hardest, way of sanctification, with little fear of deception. It is the certain following of Christ: "He hath done all things well." - *S. Mark* 7. 37.

26. *Tiny Things.*

I noticed a tone of despondency in your letter, a yielding to that commonest of all the evil suggestions of the tempter, *Cui bono?* What is the use of all this struggling without any result, and so much prayer followed by no apparent improvement? It is a very clever temptation, and a successful one with most souls, resulting in the giving up of the very things which are slowly but surely making them saints. If only one could grasp this fact: Every tiny thing (aspiration, self-denial, etc.,) makes us holier than we were. Just think of the thousands of tiny things done each day for God, *e.g.* each step we take; all is done for Him, every one of them has added to our merit, making us more pleasing in His sight, and each moment holier. No one can see this gradual spiritual growth, though sometimes when we have gained a big victory, such as the secret one you won recently over yourself, we wonder where the strength came from to do it. I have watched your steady progress in perfection with the greatest joy and gratitude for your generosity, and so I want to warn you not to listen to such a suggestion that your efforts have been in vain. Your biggest fault at present, my child, is that you have not yet completely bent your will to God's designs. I think it would please Him immensely to have no wishes of our own, apart from holy ones, so that He could bend and twist and fashion us just as He pleases, knowing well that we will not even murmur. Remember this does not mean that our *feelings* will die also.

27. *The Helping Hand.*

Don't be stingy in giving praise particularly with the young.

If in a community there is some sister not as edifying as she might be, but who after retreat makes an effort to rise, be ever the one to encourage and to hold out a helping hand. Many a first attempt has been crushed in the bud by the contemptuous look or sneering remark as to how long it will last.

28. *Humility is always safe.*

There is one thing we need never be afraid of, namely, that the devil will ever tempt us to be humble. He may delude us in the practice of other virtues; indiscreet zeal, for instance, or the desire to devote our time solely to prayer. But we need never be in doubt as to whether it would be better to humble ourselves or not. There can be no doubt about it. It is always safe to do so.

29. *Going against Ourselves.*

"If any man will come after Me, let him deny himself and take up his cross, and follow Me." - *Matthew* 16. 24. With S. Peter we tell our Lord that we will follow Him; and the first time an occasion of going against ourselves turns up, we turn our back upon Him: This saying is hard, can't do it. And yet this conquest of self is the following of Christ.

There is a certain amount of glory attached to great acts of mortification, but the little ones known only to God and ourselves are much harder to practise because of their very continuance. There is some satisfaction about the big trials, they are quickly over and attract attention. The tiny acts of self-denial are always with us.

30.

Why are we not saints? What else did we come here for? Want of courage and want of patience. We give up, we have not the strength of will and determination to succeed which the saints had. Another point is that our notion of sanctity is adding on, instead of making perfect what we already do.

<h2 style="text-align:center">31.</h2>

By entering religion and taking my vows I have given myself over absolutely to God and His service. He, therefore, has a right to be served in the way He wishes. If then He asks me to enter on a hard, mortified life and spend myself working for Him, how can I resist His will and desire? "Oh my God, make me a saint, and I consent to suffer all You ask for the rest of my life." What is God asking from me now? Shall I go back on that offering?

[1] "God calls me to an austere life; I must prepare myself to follow the ways of God."

September

1. *Reasons why our Communions and Masses do not make us Saints.*

1. Want of preparation, through sloth, careless ness, or absorption in other things; no thought of the greatness and immense dignity of the act, no stirring up of fervour. 2. No pains to examine our conscience carefully, to destroy affection to venial sin, and to root out faults often unrecognized for years. A soul filled with venial sin has no hunger for Christ. "Let a man prove himself and so let him eat this Bread," says S. Paul. 3. Routine. "Many there are who sleep," for getting that one good Communion could make them saints.

2. *Two Patron Saints.*

Two wings by which we can fly to God and become saints: the habit of little tiny acts of self-denial and the habit of making a definite fixed number of aspirations every day.

There are two patron saints to whom I have a tremendous devotion: a sheet of paper and a lead pencil. Mark down at least once a day everything you do and every time you do it. It will not make you proud to see all you do; but it will humble you by showing you all you don't do.

My dear child or should I say dear Sister Goose? your letter was a real pleasure to me, my only regret being that my reply must be a hasty one...To me at least there is no mystery why our Lord loves you so much He always loves the *generous soul*, and you have given Him proof time after time of this. Do not think because temptation still continues that you are wanting in His spirit. He leaves this craving with you in order to give Him a daily proof of the love, the much real love and affection, there is in that old heart of yours.

What a grand victory you won over the Old Boy that time! For once in my life I positively had pity for him; he must have felt so sore and humiliated.

You must absolutely drive away all despondency or useless pining or regrets about the past. It does not please God and it only injures your spiritual life.

4. *The Big Penance.*

For the present do not increase your corporal penances. You do not say anything about mortification at meals; in quantity there must be none, or not often; as regards quality you need not be so particular. But the big penance must be the joyful embracing, for the love of suffering Jesus, of the many little hard and painful things which come to you hourly. Take them all from His hand sweetly, trying to seek the unpleasant things and the hard disagreeable things; and keep hammering away at the tiny acts of self-denial. This is the goal to aim at: I am never to do a thing I like. Don't try to do that at present it might easily dishearten and crush you but keep it always in view. I would like you to keep count of these little acts like the aspirations; but Don't go too fast at first; build up and do not pull down.

5. *Indifference.*

To be indifferent does not mean to desire things which are hard to nature, but a readiness and determination to embrace them when once the will of God is known. In this sense I think I am indifferent about going to the Congo. But I must force myself to be willing to accept the way of life which God seems to be leading me to and wants me to adopt. My God, I dread it but "not my will but Thine."

6. *Venial Sin.*

How little I think of committing venial sin, and how soon I forget I have done so! Yet God hates nothing more than even the shadow of sin, nothing does more harm to my spiritual progress and hinders any real advance in holiness. My God, give me an intense hatred and dread and horror of the smallest sin. I want to please You and love You and serve You as I have never done before. Let me begin by stamping out all sin in my soul.

We could not take pleasure in living in the company of one whose body is one running, festering sore; neither can God draw us close to Himself, caress and love us, if our souls are covered with venial sin, more loathsome and horrible in His eyes than the most foul disease. To avoid mortal sin I must carefully guard against deliberate venial sin, so to avoid venial sin I must fly from the shadow of imperfection in my actions. How often in the past have I done things when I did not know if they were sins or only deliberate imperfections and how little I cared, my God!

7.

The reason I find it so hard to love God, why I have so little affection for Him, is because of my attachment to venial sin and my constant deliberate imperfections. I have, as it were, been trying to run with an immense weight round my feet; I have tried to reach the unitive way without passing through the purgative, to jump to the top of the ladder without climbing up the steps; so that after all these years I am still as barren of real love of God as when first I entered religion. No, I must work earnestly now to remove the very shadow of sin from my life, then to imitate the humble suffering life of Jesus and thus win His love.

I look upon it as a great grace that in spite of my tepid life Jesus has given me an ardent desire to love Him. I long eagerly to love my Jesus passionately, with an intense ardent love such as the saints had; and yet I remain cold and indifferent, with little zeal for His glory.

8.

You must not be afraid of what is passing in your soul. It is what I have been hoping and looking for. Were you to tell me that you were inundated with sweetness and consolation, I should have been disappointed, since you would seem to be missing the immense graces that come to you from this scourging of God's loving hand. Try to remember that what is happening is a mark of love, not of anger. "Whom the Lord loveth He chastiseth and He scourgeth every son whom He receiveth." - *Heb.* 12. 6. The inner sanctuary of God's love is set round, as it were, with a thick hedge of sharp thorns. No wonder when one tries to force one's way through it and the thorns pierce to the very heart, human nature should cry out, and, alas! too often weakly turn back from the only road that leads to pure love; no wonder indeed, for this painful struggling, every step of which is, as it were, marked with blood, seems to anger Jesus and drive Him further away. But courage! He is only "pretending," to test the valiant lover, and soon the sweets of victory will well repay the hardness of the fight.

9. *S. Peter Claver.*

S. Peter Claver was one of those generous heroic souls whom God sends upon this earth to serve as a stimulus to our zeal, to urge us on to dare and do great things for His glory. Alone he stood upon the beach of that reeking haunt of sin, Cartagena, and saw the galley-ship vomit forth its human living burden of slaves. He saw these poor wretches dazed with their long confinement, sick in body and weary of soul, cast on the burning sand, their eyes wild with terror at the vision of the nameless death they thought awaited them. Here was scope for his zeal. Was not the image of Jesus stamped deep upon the souls of each of them? Did they not bear the likeness of the sacred Humanity in their tortured limbs? Was this goodly harvest to be left ungathered and hell alone to reap the fruit of man's cupidity?

10. *Ordinary Daily Actions.*

It seems to me the best and most practical resolution I can make in this retreat is to deter mine to perform each action with the greatest perfection. This will mean a constant "going against self," ever *agendo contra,* at every moment and every single day. I have a vast field to cover in my ordinary daily actions, *e.g.* to say the Angelus always with the utmost attention and fervour. I feel, too, that Jesus asks this from me, as without it there can be no real holiness.

11. *Zeal for Souls.*

My intense desire and longing is to make others love Jesus and to draw them to His Sacred Heart. Recently at Mass I have found myself at the *Dominus Vobiscum* opening my arms wide with the intention of embracing every soul present and drawing them in spite of themselves into that Heart which longs for their love. "Compel them to come in," Jesus said. Yes, compel them to dive into that abyss of love. Sometimes, I might say nearly always, when speaking to people I am seized with an extra ordinary desire to draw their hearts to God. I could go down on my knees before them and beg them to be pure and holy, so strong do I feel the longing of Jesus for sanctity in everyone, and since I may not do this, I try to do what I find hard to describe in words to pour out of my heart any grace or love of God there may be in it, and then with all the force of my will to draw their hearts into that of Jesus.

12.

If I do not begin to serve God as I ought now, when shall I do so? shall I ever? This retreat is a time of special grace, and if my cooperation is wanting, Jesus may pass by and not return. The devil has made me put off my thorough conversion for seventeen years, making me con tent myself with the resolution of "later on really beginning in earnest and becoming a saint." What might not have been done in that time!

13. *The Object of Life.*

I realise in a way I never did before that God created me for His service, that He has a strict right that I should serve Him perfectly, and that every moment of my life is His and given to me for the one end of praising and serving Him. I recall with horror how often I have wandered from this my end, what an appalling amount of time I have wasted, and how few of my actions were done for God or worthy of being offered to Him. I see what I should have been and what I am. But the thought of Jesus waiting and eagerly looking out for me, the prodigal, during fifteen years, has filled me with hope and confidence and new resolve to turn to my dearest Jesus and give Him all He asks.

I have begun to try to perform each little action with great fervour and exactness, having as my aim to get back the fervour of my first year's noviti-ate.

15. *The Happiness of Religious Life.*

Well the "plunge" is over, and though I know you must feel a little lonely after the pain of parting, I am certain you are not sorry you were so brave. That happiness and contentment will grow more and more as the days go on, and you come to realise better the meaning and the grandeur of religious life, a life which is "all for Jesus" and His interests, without a thought of self. Then the happiness of knowing that the same roof shelters both you and our Blessed Lord, that He is really one of the Community, and that a few steps will bring you to His feet for consolation and help when the cross is heavy and the clouds are black. Yes, my child, Jesus has been loving and good to you; so good that you cannot sound the depths of His tenderness and never can repay Him unless by giving Him the love of all your heart and striving to refuse Him nothing. If you take these two words as the motto of your life: "love and generosity," they will carry you far on the path of perfection.

16. *Keep at it.*

Try to grasp the fact (a very hard thing to do), that in the spiritual life "feelings" count for nothing, that they are no indication of our real state. Generally speaking, they point to just the opposite. When I feel I am making no progress and not pleasing our Lord the absence of deliberate sin being sup-posed the opposite is nearly always the case.

Hammer this into your little head, try and convince yourself of it: Our Blessed Lord love me, with all my faults and failings, and has marked *me* out for the special graces which will make *me* a saint, a big one if I like. I could give you proofs in abundance if I had time. Any other thought - *e.g.* it is use-less, presumption, trying to be a saint - is a dangerous temptation to be driv-en away. You are bound to go through a good deal of weariness, dryness, doubt, despair even of ever doing anything towards this end; but one day the truth of your high vocation will burst upon you.

With this ideal before you, which you must reach if God's plans are not to be spoiled, try and remember that sanctification means daily, hourly, *hard work,* and this unflinchingly, when weariness comes.

17. *Danger of Overwork.*

A deadly pitfall lies hidden in the desire of some to pour themselves out in works of zeal for God's glory, to which the evil spirit not uncommonly urges those whom he sees full of zeal. It is evident even to one little versed in the way of the spiritual life that a multiplicity of external occupations, even though good and meritorious in themselves, must by their very nature hinder that calm peace of soul which is essential for interior union with God.

For one who has advanced in the way of interior union, no life, no matter how occupied or full of distracting work, will prove much of a hindrance; such a one has learned how to ride on the waves of worldly care and not to be engulfed by them, he refuses to put himself out or be totally absorbed in things which have only a fleeting interest; but it is not so with the beginner in the spiritual life. Overwork has broken down not a few weakly bodies but has ruined far more souls, drying up if not destroying all love for prayer and the things of God, leaving the wreck of many a "spoiled saint" strewn on the road of life.

A heavy responsibility rests on the souls of those who heap an impossible burden on the shoulders of the "willing horse," more anxious for the material success of their particular charitable undertaking than for the spiritual progress of those whom God has entrusted to their care.

18. *God's Presence.*

Without constant union with our Lord there cannot be any real holiness, one reason being that without recollection the inspirations of the Holy Spirit are missed and with them a host of opportunities of little sacrifices and a shower of graces. As a means of gaining greater recollection, each morning at Holy Communion invite Jesus to dwell in your heart during the day as in a Tabernacle. Try all day to imagine even His bodily presence within you and often turn your thoughts inwards and adore Him as He nestles next your heart in a very real manner, quite different from His presence in all creation. This habit is not easily acquired, especially in a busy life like yours, but much may be done by constant effort. At times you will have to leave Him alone entirely, but as soon as you can, get back to His presence again.

19. *The Fault of Overwinding One's Faults.*

Our dear Lord is certainly testing the extent of your love for Him before He takes you to Himself. But should not that make you rejoice, my dear child, since the harder and sharper the fight, the closer will be your union with Him in heaven? I have just one fault to blame you for: you have always kept your eyes fixed on your faults - I do not deny there are plenty! - and have never helped yourself by thinking on what you have done and suffered for His dear sake. If you have forgotten all this, He has not; and when you meet Him, the gratitude of His loving Heart will hide the imperfections and faults of former years. Be brave and generous to the end, my dear child, and do not take back what He asks you to give, though He knew well what it would cost you.

20. *Devotion to the Holy Ghost.*

A devotion which does not consist in any special form of prayer nor in doing anything in particular more than to listen to inspirations, is devotion to the Holy Spirit of God. And does it not commend itself very specially to religious? For, as the work of Creation belongs pre-eminently to the Father and that of Redemption to the Son, so the work of our Sanctification and Perfection is the work of the Holy Ghost. We honour Him when we listen to His inspirations. He is ever whispering what we ought to do and what we ought not to do. When we are deliberately deaf to His voice, which is no other than the small voice of conscience, we grieve instead of honouring the Holy Spirit of God. So let us often say: Come O Holy Ghost into my heart and make me holy so that I may be generous with God and become a saint. See what the Holy Spirit made of the Apostles changed them from skulking cowards into great saints afire with the love of God.

21. *Wholehearted Love.*

We must love God with our whole heart. Can He be loved otherwise? Is it too much that a finite heart should love infinite Beauty? I fail in this wholehearted love if I keep back anything from Him, if I am determined not to pass certain limits as proof of my love, if I absolutely refuse to sacrifice certain things which He asks, if I refuse to follow the grace which is impelling me on. It is not necessary to imagine extraordinary circumstances in the future; there is presumption in this; we must not count on ourselves as S. Peter did. Also there is a danger of despondency in such imaginings, when we do not feel capable of such tests of love. Examine the present.

We must love God with our whole strength. If I love God with all the strength that grace gives me now, this grace is increased by each act of love, so that I should from day to day love Him more. Love for a creature is strongest at its commencement, it becomes weaker, it ends in weariness and disgust. It is quite the contrary with divine love. Weak in the beginning, it grows as we come to know God better, as we taste Him more, as we approach Him more familiarly and enjoy His presence more intimately.

22. *All from God.*

You know well that even the smallest cross and happening of your life is part of our Blessed Lord's plan for your sanctification. It is not easy, I know, to look at things in this light. But one can train the will to look upon the act of others, even their sinful acts in as much as they concern ourselves, as coming from the hand of God. There is so much real holiness and so very much solid happiness and peace and contentment in this little principle, that I am very anxious you should try and acquire it, so that nothing may really ruffle the peace of your soul. Don t think this is easy, it is not; and you will fail time after time in your efforts, but with perseverance, steady progress will be made.

23. *Daily Self-Conquest.*

It is indeed easy to condemn oneself to death, to make a generous offering of self-immolation; but to carry out the execution daily is more than most can do....Go on bravely, Don't expect too much from yourself, for God often leaves one powerless in acts of self-conquest in order to make one humble and to have more recourse to Him. Remember above all that even one small victory makes up for a hundred defects.

24.

You may make the most complete and absolute offering of yourself to God to bear every pain He may wish to send. Renew this frequently and place yourself in His hands as His willing victim to be immolated on the altar of sacrifice. But it is better not to ask directly for great sufferings; few of the saints did so.

25.

"My yoke is sweet." - *S. Matthew* 11. 30. The service of God, the whole-hearted generous service of God, is full of a sweetness hidden from the world. Beneath the rough garb of the monk or the holy nun's coarse garment there is hidden more real happiness, more true peace and contentment than poor wordlings have ever known or dreamt of. Sweet is the yoke, light the burden of the Lord.

26.

How much is comprised in the little words *agere contra!* Therein is the real secret of sanctity, the hidden source from which the saints have drunk deep of the love of God and reached that height of glory they now enjoy.

27.

For fifteen years has Jesus been waiting for me to return to Him, to return to the fervour of my first year of religious life. During that time how many pressing and loving invitations has He not given me? What lights and inspirations, remorse of conscience, and how many good resolves which were never carried into effect. O my God, I feel now as if I cannot resist You longer. Your infinite patience and desire to bring me to You has broken the ice of my cold heart. "I will arise and go" to You, humbled and sorrowful, and for the rest of my life give You of my very best. Help me, sweet Jesus, by Your grace, for I am weak and cowardly.

28.

I have been thinking much over all these crosses. And the more I think the happier I become. This sounds heartless, but let me explain. You remember your offering to be God's Victim and how you gave yourself up without reserve into His hands to do what He pleased with you, your sole condition being that He would make you a saint, cost what it might. I know you do not regret that heroic offering and later on you will rejoice with all your heart that you made it.

From that time your big "troubles" graces, I call them began...What does it all mean? Simply this, my child, that God has heard your prayer and accepted your sacrifice and this should make your heart bound with joy He means to give you graces beyond your wildest dreams and lift you to a high degree of holiness. This He could never do until you were crushed, until the "grain of wheat" was dead and not merely buried. I fancy, my child, there was far more secret, hidden pride in your nature than you ever realized or I suspected, though there were many little signs here and there; for example, the difficulty you found in letting your self be walked on, the way you felt humiliations etc. Then God in His love put you under the mill and crushed you by suffering and disappointments and humiliations, till He humbled you and made you see that self and self-will must go and His will alone be your wish and desire.

This is not to be a kind of resigned, or perhaps rebellious, conformity; but a generous cheerful, though not felt, embracing of what He wills.

Do you wonder I am glad and daily thank God for His goodness to you and the promise there is of future things? Don't let the devil spoil the work by making you fret and worry.

29. *Be "Put Out" by Nothing.*

Try to grasp the fact a very hard thing to do that in the spiritual life feelings count for nothing, that they are no indication of our real state; generally speaking they are just the opposite....You are perfectly right when you say that the first thing to do is to give up you own will. Why not aim at making God's will alone yours in every detail of life, so that you would never desire or wish for anything except what He willed, and look on every detail as coming from His hand, as it does? Such a one is never "put out" by anything bad weather, unpleasant work, annoying incidents, they are all His doing and His sweet will. Try it, though it means high perfection.

30. *A Birthday Letter.*

You know my earnest wish and prayer for you this morning: *Ad multos annos,* to do more each day for the dear Master who has been so good to us all.

Fifty years of life means much merit heaped up and many souls saved; for although when we look back on the past we see many a fault and many a grace neglected or opportunity let slip, still the consoling thought comes that every moment of our religious life, at least, has been freely given to Him. If He has promised a reward for even a cup of water, what may we not expect for the many hard days patiently borne and generous things done for His love? Don t dwell on what you have not done, for I think that want of confidence in His willingness to forgive our shortcomings pains Him very much, but rather *Sursum corda,* lift up your heart and think what you are going to do for Him now. You know the secret of making a short life very long in His eyes, and a life of few opportunities crammed full of precious things. Do everything for His sweet love alone.

October

1. *The Rosary.*

To Mary's feet in heaven to-day the angels come in never-ending stream to lay before her the offerings of her loving earthly children. To their Queen they bear fair wreaths of lovely roses. In many a lonely cottage or amid the bustle of the great city have these crowns been formed. Little ones and old folk, the pious nun and holy priest, the sinner too and many a wandering soul, have added to the glory of the Queen of Heaven; and from every corner of this earth to-day has risen the joyous praise of her who is Queen of the Holy Rosary. On earth she was the lowly handmaid of the Lord, and now all generations proclaim the greatness of her name.

2. *Some Resolutions of Fr. Doyle (2nd Feb., 1909).*

With the boys absolute meekness, gentleness, and patience.
Never speak about your worries, troubles, amount of work.
Do not let an unkind, angry or uncharitable word pass your lips.
Don't complain of others or of anything else.
Always be punctual.
Great fidelity to your own order of time, doing everything at the hour fixed.

If possible say all the Office on your knees before the Blessed Sacrament.

Never give yourself relief in small sufferings.

When in pain or unwell, try and not let others know it. Hence never say you have a head ache, etc.

You have promised never deliberately to waste a moment of time.

Be very observant about the rule of silence.

The constant mortification of intense fervour at each little duty.

In general: (*a*) never do anything you would like; (*b*) deny yourself every gratification; (*c*) deny yourself every pleasure; (*d*) do the thing *because* it is hard; (*e*) in all things *agere contra.*

3. *Our Angel Guardian.*

A little child is born into this world and as it opens its eyes for the first time to God's blessed light, swiftly a heavenly messenger descends and unseen how often too unthought of takes his place beside the cot of that tiny babe. He hath given His angels charge over us, to guide us, to guard and shelter us from dangers, to lead us safely through this world of sin and bring us to the throne prepared for us in heaven. Ever beside us our faithful angel stays. We heed him not; his spotless purity, his majestic dignity, checks us not in our career of sin; but could we see our guardian spirit when passion urges us on, the sight would check our downward path.

4. *God's Chisel.*

I can quite understand your difficult position and the suffering caused I can quite believe unintentionally by the Sister you speak of. .... Once get hold of the principle that all that happens comes straight from the hand of God, and you have found the secret of deep peace which nothing can disturb. You must look upon this Sister as the "chisel" in the Almighty Worker's hand. He knows the best tool to use, and all we have to do is to let Him use it as He pleases. Don't expect that poor weak human nature will submit to the blows without a murmur. But with an effort of the will we can crush this down, until in the end what once caused us pain and tears becomes the source of great interior joy, since we have realised how these things help on our spiritual progress. Hence I would advise you without any hesitation, not to try to get a change unless it be to a house where you will have *two* disagreeable Sisters instead of one! This may sound a bit heroic, but...there is no happiness like seeking and embracing the "hard things" for the love of Jesus.

5. *"I am no Saint."*

S. Bona venture gives in four short sentences the epitome of the Third Degree of Humility: to despise the world, to despise no one, to despise oneself, to wish to be despised. And all the saints have done this. Let us never forget that they did not do these things because they were saints, but the doing of these things made them saints.

Do I ever say, when an occasion of denying myself comes, "It's too hard, I am no saint?" Might it not be asked of me in justice, "Why aren't you? It is your business to be one, God intends you should be one, but you are too lazy, you won't take the trouble."

Let us remember that we must not drag Christ down to our own level, but rather we must let Christ lift us up to His level.

6. *Christ's Visit to the Soul.*

"Behold I stand at the gate and knock." - *Apoc.* 3. 20.

Jesus stands at the door of my heart, patiently, uncomplainingly. How long has He been there? A year? Ten years? I have been afraid to let Him in.

Jesus knocks: "Open to Me, My Beloved." My heart has been closed fast in spite of His calls, His inspirations, the appeals of His grace. How long? I have heard Him knocking, I have pretended I did not, I have longed He would go away. My God, how I must have pained You; but do not go away, wait a little longer.

I look out timidly to see who is calling. Why should I be afraid to let *Him* in? He has come to me, I have not sought Him. What love He must have for me! Jesus, why am I afraid of You, afraid to let You come into my heart?

7.

Solid virtue is so called because it is formed by amassing together a facility in repeated acts. Hence the practice of any virtue is not the less meritorious because it is easy. Quite the contrary. The merit depends on the intention we had when we determined to practise the virtue, and not on the amount of pain it costs.

8.

You do not pain me by telling me of your inmost thoughts. I thank God that He gives you the strength to perform that act of humility which must cost much but will certainly draw down graces on your soul. A nun told me once that for years she was never able to rise promptly, but never failed to do so from the day she told this fault to her superior with whom she was most anxious to stand well. The only thing which would pain me would be sin of any kind. But these thoughts do not displease God one bit, they help you to realise how miserable and wretched you are when left to yourself.

9. *Prayer for Sinners.*

Pray for all, but especially for sinners, and in particular for those whose sins are most painful to His Sacred Heart. With great earnestness recommend to His mercy the poor souls who are in their agony. What a dreadful hour, an hour tremendously decisive, is the hour of our death! Surround with your love these souls going to appear before God, and defend them by your prayers.

10. *Do not Rush.*

Avoid haste and want of control of bodily movements. The interior man, no matter how burdened with work or pressed for time, is never in a hurry. He is swift and expeditious in all he does, but never rushes; and by a jealous watch fulness over odd moments, "gathering up the fragments" of a full day "that none of them may be lost," he finds time for all things. He knows that the Almighty is never in a hurry; that the great works of God in nature as in the soul are done silently and calmly, and that there is much wisdom in the old monastic saying, "The man who rushes will never run to perfection."

11.

If the rule is not observed, God will not accept any other external work we may do for Him. Take silence for example, how lightly that rule is snapped, and yet it is a rule.

Let us love silence and recollection. When we are at home with silence we are at home with God.

Silence seems impossible to busy people. But "silence of the heart," interior silences, is always possible.

12.

We never know how many people are so keenly interested in our future happiness, so anxious to warn us of the difficulties and dangers of our proposed step, until it becomes known we are entering religion.

Endless harm has been done by well-meaning people, who under pretext of "trying a vocation," keep their children from entering religion for years.

13.

My victory over myself, my inclinations, is a victory won for the cause of Jesus. I have been a deserter to the camp of Satan, a traitor; but now my King has pardoned me and received me back. How am I going to show my gratitude and make up for the past which I cannot recall the time lost, duties omitted or done without love or fervour, little sacrifices refused, my many,

many sins? Shall I not be busy at every hour, fighting for my King, gaining victory after victory over the enemy, over myself? My Jesus, help me now to work for You, to slave for You, to fight for You, and then *to die* for You!

14.

Perseverance is what God wants. If we get up and start again after *each* fall, God *will* make saints of us in the end.

15. *S. Teresa.*

The life of S. Teresa teaches us that we should never despair of becoming saints. As a child she was filled with a strange mysterious longing for martyrdom. But the early years of her religious life found her cold or tepid in the service of God, indifferent to the sacred duties of her state. The call came. Sweetly in her ear sounded that little voice which too often in other souls has been hushed and stifled. Teresa rose. The past was gone and no lamenting could recall its ill-spent days, but the present was hers, and the future lay before her. Ungenerous in the past, generosity would be her darling virtue; cold and careless, no one would now equal her burning love for her patient outraged Saviour.

16.

To stay on your feet when you have a bad headache may be even heroic and is not likely to injure you in any way. What a love the saints all had for suffering! There must be something in it.

17. *The Office.*

The Office is the grandest prayer we can say, since it is the public prayer of the Church. It is *opus Dei,* the work of God.

Two motives should always be present when we recite the Office: to glorify God and to implore mercy for sinners.

We should have the intention of praying. It does not matter if we cannot understand what we are saying God does.

18. *Time for Recollection.*

You seem to have fallen into the common snare of Satan, namely, mistaking your work for prayer and pouring yourself out over it. Thus the soul gets dried up and the body so fatigued that a proper service of God is impossible. Give the full time to spiritual duties. Try to get a minute to yourself, and a half hour on Sundays, and walk about quietly and examine your state. Note where you have fallen off, etc., and begin again, instead of waiting for the next retreat to pull you up.

19. *How to Conquer Worries.*

Try to draw closer each day the bonds of union with Him, thinking often of His dwelling within your soul, and so making your heart beat in union with His; that is, seeking and wishing for only His adorable will in all things, even the smallest. This will conquer all worries, for nothing which comes from the loving hand of God can ever be a worry to us.

20. *Loving Trust.*

This morning during Mass I felt strongly that Jesus was pained that you do not trust Him absolutely, that is, trust Him in every detail of your life. You are wanting in that childlike confidence He desires so much from you, the taking lovingly and trustfully from His hands all that He sends you, not even wishing things to have happened otherwise. He wants you to possess your soul in peace in the midst of the many troubles, cares and difficulties of your work, looking upon everything as arranged by Him, and hence something to welcome joyfully. Jesus will not dwell in your soul as He wishes unless you are at peace. This is the first step towards that union which you desire so much but not so much as He does. Don't keep Him waiting, my child, but by earnest and constant efforts empty your heart of every care that He may abide with you for ever.

21.

A holy nun is kneeling motionless before the altar of a little convent chapel. She is alone, for the night is well advanced and gentle sleep has laid her hand upon the weary brows of the pious sisterhood. Fitfully the pale light of the sanctuary lamp rises and falls, shedding its soft rays upon the Tabernacle door where dwells the silent Prisoner of Love. Long hours of sweet converse have passed between the kneeling spouse and Him she loves so well, hours of time, long weary hours to a poor distracted being but to her a few short moments of heavenly ecstasy. Jesus is near, her Jesus, the beloved of pious hearts, He who feeds among the lilies.

22.

"If Thou wilt, Thou canst make me clean." - *S. Matthew* 8. 2. Jesus loves to be trusted. He hides His greatness and His power from us that we may ask our favours with boundless faith, confident that He can do far more than what we ask. At times He seems to be heedless of our petitions and leaves our prayers unanswered long, but it is only to try our confidence and that we may seek Him with more earnestness.

23. *Nothing is Too Small.*

I think He would like you to pay more attention to *little things,* looking on nothing as small, if connected with His service and worship. Also try to remember that nothing is too small too small to offer to Him that is, the tiniest act of self-conquest is of immense value in His eyes, and even lifting one's eyes as an act of love brings great grace.

24. *The Last Judgement.*

"Render an account of thy stewardship!" - *S. Luke* 16. 2. To all of us these words must yet be spoken. Shall we hear them from the lips of an angry God, words full of awful menace for the treasures which we have squandered? Will they come to us in gentle reproach from a loving Master, in tones of meek rebuke for a life of wasted opportunities? Or will this summons fill our hearts with holy joy, that now the world may see and know how well we have kept our trust, how faithfully served, how generously toiled for Him who gave us all? Or what will be our feelings when too late the thought of all we might have done for Jesus will burst upon us? How little it would have cost us to have loved Him more and served Him better!

25. *Fr. Doyle's Offering of Himself. (25th Oct. 1907).*

God has been very good to me in enlightening my mind to see His will and in filling my heart with a most ardent desire to do it cost what it may. Jesus, dear Jesus, I want to please You, to do exactly what You want of me, to give all generously this time without any reserve, and never to go back on my resolution. In this spirit I made the midnight meditation on October 25th, the Feast of B. Margaret Mary. I saw clearly what I knew r years ago, but would not admit: that God is asking from me the practice of the Third Degree [1] in all its perfection as far as I am capable. I cannot deny it or shut my eyes to this truth any longer. Should i not be grateful to the good God for choosing me for such a life, since it will be all the work of His grace and not my own doing? -God wants me to put perfection sanctity before me and to "go straight" for that, for holiness. He wants me not to be content with the ordinary good life of the average religious, but to aim at something higher, nobler, more worthy of Him. He wants me to make ceaseless war on myself, my passions, inclinations, habits; to smash and break down my own will, to mortify it in all things so that it may be free for His grace to act upon; in a word, to aim at the perfection of the Third Degree and all that that means, not for one day or month or a year, but for the rest of my life, faithfully, unceasingly, constantly, *without rest or intermission.* To do this I must strive to cut away all comfort in my life, choose that which is "hard," go against my natural inclination, and give up the easy self-indulgent life I have hitherto led. The motive for this is the immense, deep, real love of the Heart of Jesus for *me,* His example which He wants me to follow, for He chose want of all things, suffering and a hard, comfortless life, and by doing the same I imitate Him and become more and more like to Him. Can I do this for five, ten, twenty years lead a crucified life so long? Jesus does not ask that, but only that I do so for *this day* so quickly passed and with it the recollection of the little suffering and mortifications endured once over, all is over, but the eternal reward remains.

My Jesus, I feel that at last You have conquered, Your love has conquered; and last night, kneeling before the image of Your Sacred Heart, I promised You to begin this new life, to begin at last to serve You as You urged me to do during the past sixteen years. I made my promise, knowing well my weakness, but trusting in Your all-powerful grace to do what seems almost impossible to my cowardly nature. *Ego dixi: nunc coepi.* I promise You, sweet Jesus, to serve You perfectly with all the fervour of my soul, aiming at the Third Degree in its perfection. I make this offering through the hands of B. Margaret Mary. Amen.

26. *Flesh versus Spirit.*

You need not be uneasy to see in your soul apparent contradictions: an ardent desire to love God and to suffer for Him, and then when the opportunity comes, a shrinking from pain, and even a refusal to bear it. Fortunately we are dealing with our Lord who can read the heart and who knows our protestations of love are sincere and genuine, with One, too, who knows the weakness of our human nature and who does not expect much from us. He does not forget His own human weakness on earth. "With desire have I desired to eat this Pasch with you before I suffer," He said, showing His longing for His Passion. And then an hour after He seems to take His offering back: "Father, if it be possible, let this chalice pass from Me." The very longing to love Him and bear much for His sake is dear to our Lord, even if our courage fails when tested.

27.

"At Thy rebuke they shall flee." - *Ps.* 103. 7. Far from the face of an angry God the damned shall flee to bury themselves for a miserable eternity in the depths of hell. Better far the scorching fire and maddening pain, than to stand before that Saviour once so loving and so merciful, whom they have outraged.

28.

Every grace we get enlightens the understanding and strengthens the will. When the understanding is enlightened, we have the awful alternative of co-operating with or rejecting the inspirations of grace. This we are either doing or not doing all the day long. God will not compel us, He will not interfere with our freedom, it must be our own choice. S. Paul was struck down when he received the inspiration. But he did not lie there as so many of us do. He got up and asked God what He wanted him to do. His will was strengthened because he accepted the grace that was offered. Let us do the same. From neglect of Thy holy inspirations, O Lord, deliver us.

29.

"Time that passeth like a shadow." *Ecclesiastes,* 7. 1. Watch the shadow of the sun's rays creep silently across the dial's face. Slowly, irresistibly it moves on. No power of man can stay its course; the fair, the mighty, the eloquent, may plead in vain, but nought can check its onward march; ever relentlessly forward man's destiny is hastening to its end.

30. *A Lay-Brother Saint.*

S. Alphonsus Rodriguez is a striking example of one who, though in a lowly station in life, devoid of all that in the eyes of the world makes for greatness, yet did a mighty work for God. With a heart burning with zeal, which prayer alone could not satisfy, he saw in the young ardent Peter Claver a ready instrument for the work he longed to do. With burning words he fires the soul of the future apostle with a hunger for abandoned souls. He tells him of the wretched slaves dragging out a miserable existence in a far-off world, knowing not the name of Jesus; he pictures to him the rich and golden harvest to be reaped, the victories over sin and Satan; he whispers of the pain and suffering, the heat, the toil, the lingering death, till Claver's heart is aflame with zeal, burning with a holy fire.

With tender love did the old saint watch the young one grow in virtue day by day; with trembling hands he begs that grace may fall upon this fresh ardent soul and make him worthy of the heavenly call. Alphonsus's eyes soon must close in death, his time is nearly run, his hour of sweet repose is drawing near; but if he may no longer toil for God, at least he longs to leave behind him one whom by his prayers and bright example he has made a saint.

31. *S. Peter's Fall.*

S. Peter relied too much on himself; it was always 'I will do this' and 'I will do that.' If he had said: 'Lord, I know my own weakness, but I'll do it with *Your* help' - it would have been quite different.

The servant maid asked Peter if he were a follower of Jesus and he denied Him. Have we ever been asked if we were a follower of Christ, a religious? Perhaps we replied: Oh, yes! But did not our life give the lie to our words? How often have we denied our crucified Master, whom we vowed to follow, when the hard thing came and we refused to make the sacrifice.

Let us beg of Jesus to look on us as He looked on Peter and to fill our hearts with sorrow for the past and with humility, love and confidence in Him for the future.

[1] "The third degree is the most perfect humility; when...the better to imitate Christ our Lord and to become actually more like to Him, I desire and choose poverty with Christ poor rather than riches, contempt with Christ contemned rather than honours.... "Spiritual Exercises of S. Ignatius."

November

1. *The Heroism of the Saints.*

Heroism is a virtue which has an attraction for every heart. It seems to lift us out of our petty selves and make us for a moment forget our own selfish interests. It appeals irresistibly to the noble-minded; even to the cowardly it is a powerful stimulus. Thus it is that in all times the saints have ever had such an attraction for men they are heroes! In their secret hidden lives of prayer and penance men saw a heroism which was not the one sharp pang of a fearless deed, leaving their names to history as a nation's pride, but the nobler heroism of a life of countless noble deeds, unknown perhaps to man; by God alone were their secret victories seen.

2. *The Souls in Purgatory.*

From their cleansing prison of fire the holy souls cry to us for help. With joy indeed they bear the pain which cleanses them from the foul marks of sin, for now at last they know the awful purity of Him against whom on earth they dared to sin. Upon their souls they see the hideous taint of what was once their joy; and even were heaven's gates thrown open wide, they would not enter and stand with spotted robe before Him in whose eyes the heavens themselves are not pure. Still they sigh and long for the happiness of their eternal home, for the company of the blessed saints, for Jesus whom at last they know. To be separated from Him is now their most grievous pain, exceeding far the torture of the cleansing fires.

3.

Solid virtue is not a mushroom plant springing up in a night, but a growth of slow and gradual development. Many forgetting this have rushed at the task of making themselves saints, but after a few days or weeks of impetuous, generous efforts, seeing no results, have concluded that sanctity was not for them.

4. *Failures.*

Our Lord is displeased only when He sees no attempt made to get rid of imperfections which, when deliberate, clog the soul and chain it to the earth. But He often purposely does not give the victory over them in order to increase our opportunities of meriting. Make an act of humility and sorrow after failure, and then never a thought more about it.

He sees what a "tiny little child" you are, and how useless even your greatest efforts are to accomplish the gigantic work of making a saint. But this longing, this stretching out of baby hands for His love, pleases Him beyond measure; and one day He will stoop down and catch you up with infinite tenderness in His divine arms and raise you to heights of sanctity you little dream of now.

5. *The Saints of the Society.*

The thought of our saints now in heaven should serve as a great encouragement to us to walk bravely in the way of holiness. On earth they led the life that we lead; there was little to distinguish them from the other members with whom they lived. Yet before God what a vast difference! How perfectly each action was per formed; with how much fervour, with what exact attention to each detail, with what intense love of God! Each moment brought its duty, each hour its allotted task; and all, both sweet and bitter, were joyfully accepted as the manifestation of the divine will in their regard. Thus the years sped swiftly by, leaving behind the sweet odour of a well-spent life and laborious days, days full of merit and crowned with victories, hard but glorious, over self.

6. *To Acquire Interior Union.*

I feel drawn still more to the life of interior union. To acquire this I must practise the following:

1. Constant and profound recollection. **2.** To keep my thoughts always if possible centred on Jesus in my heart. **3.** To avoid worry and anxiety about future things. **4.** To avoid useless conversation. **5.** Great guard over my eyes, not reading or looking at useless things.

7. *Bit by Bit.*

Try to take your days one by one as they come to you. The hard things of yesterday are past, and you are not asked to bear what to-morrow may have in store; so that the cross is really light when you take it bit by bit.

8. *Repugnances.*

These natural repugnances will not take away from the merit of the act, rather they seem to add to its merit, for our Blessed Lord permits and thereby sanctifies repugnances. We can never sufficiently thank Him for so completely showing us in the Garden that He was a man by praying to escape the storm.

God allows us to beg of Him to lessen or with draw our trial, provided that beneath all there be "Thy will be done."

9. *His Voice.*

"And the Lord came and stood; and He called as He had called the other times: Samuel, Samuel. And Samuel said: Speak, Lord, for Thy servant heareth." - 1 *Kings* 3. 10.

How often the Lord has stood by me, anxious to whisper His message, to ask me to do something for Him, and then He has gone sadly away my heart was not ready.

Lord I have heard Your voice for years, but I pretended I didn't; I persuaded myself I didn't; I forced myself to believe that what You asked, what I heard, was not Your voice.

What will You have me to do now? Speak to me, for now I am listening. Speak, Lord; do not mind my feelings, my cowardice, my shrinking from the light. My heart is ready to do Your will.

10.

Holiness and perfection depend on yourself, not on the actions of others.

11. *Death.*

Death is the end of all things here, the end of time, of merit, of pain and mortification, of a hard life. It is the commencement of an eternal life of happiness and joy. "God will wipe away all tears from their eyes." - *Apoc.* 21. 4. In this light, life is short indeed and penance sweet. I thought if I knew I had only one year to live, how fervently I would spend it, how each moment would be utilised. Yet I know well I may not live a week more do I really believe this?

12. *"Just this Once."*

Making my meditation before the picture of the Blessed Cure of Ars, he seemed to say to me with an interior voice: The secret of my life was that *I lived for the moment.* I did not say, "I must pray here for the next hour," but only "for this moment." I did not say, "I have a hundred confessions to hear," but looked upon this one as the first and last. I did not say, "I must deny myself everything and always," but only "just this once." By this means I was able always to do everything perfectly, quietly and in great peace. Try and live this life of the present moment. Pray as if you had nothing else whatever to do; say your Office slowly as if for the last time; do not look forward and think you must often repeat this act of self-denial. This will make all things much easier.

No sacrifice would be great if looked at in this way. I do not feel now the pain which has past, I have not yet to bear what is coming; hence I have only to endure the suffering of *this one moment,* which is quickly over and cannot return.

13. *Hell.*

I can imagine I am a soul in hell, and God in His mercy is saying to me, "Return to the world for this year and on your manner of life during the year will depend your returning to hell or not." What a life I should lead! How little I should think of suffering, of mortification! How I would rejoice in suffering! How perfectly each moment would be spent! If God treated me as I deserved, I should be in hell now. Shall I ever again have cause for grumbling or complaining, no matter what may happen? My habit of constantly speaking uncharitably of others, and, in general, faults of the tongue, seem to me the chief reason why I derive so little fruit from my Mass and spiritual duties. Nothing dries up the fountains of grace so much as an affection for sin.

14. *Prayer.*

You certainly put your finger on the weak spot in most priestly lives the want of prayer. The connection between prayer and zeal never struck me so forcibly before, though holy David says so truly, "In my meditation a fire shall flame oat." - *Psalm* 38. 4. As for personal holiness, you know my views on that, and how convinced I am that all work for God must in the main be barren without it.

15. *The Barren Fig-Tree.*

For sixteen years has Jesus been seeking fruit from my soul, and especially in these last three years of preparation for the priesthood. I have no excuse, for He has told me how to produce that fruit, especially by the exact discharge of each little duty of the moment. "Spare it for this year." Never shall I have this opportunity again of becoming holy; and if now I do not "dig round" this unfruitful tree so that it bear much fruit, Jesus will surely "cut it down" by withdrawing His graces and *loving invitations.*

16. *The Struggle for Perfection.*

Your difficulty is merely God's plan for your sanctification. "My child, let Me do with you what I will." [1] This is hard to submit to, especially when our Lord hides himself in the background and uses other instruments to do His work on us. Never mind, my dear child, you are making undoubted progress. Jesus may hide it from your eyes, but He does not hide it from mine. I do not trouble in the least about your little faults and failings, which will vanish as you become more perfect and grow more in the love of what is hard to nature. For your consolation remember that everyone I have ever met found the struggle for perfection hard because most of the work is done in the dark. It is a question of faith and courage, going along bravely day after day, gathering up a sacrifice here and there, and although many are let slip, every one we lay at the feet of our Lord means so much solid progress.

17. *The Great Audit.*

Meditating on the Particular Judgement, God gave me great light. I realised that I should have to give an exact account of every action of my life and for every instant of time. To take only my seventeen years of religious life, what account could I give of the 6,000 hours of meditation, 7,000 Masses, 12,000 examinations of conscience, etc.? Then my time how have I spent every moment? I resolved not to let a day more pass without seriously trying to reform my life in the manner in which I perform my ordinary daily duties. For years I have been "going to begin," and from time to time made some slight efforts at improvement. But now, dear Jesus, let this change be the work of Thy right hand.

To perform each action well I will try and do them: (*a*) with a pure intention often renewed, (*b*) *attente* earnestly, punctually exactly, (*c*) *devote* with great fervour.

18.

Your desire for penance is an excellent sign, and this in spite of what X said. But have a fixed amount to be done each day and do not be doing it in fits and starts. Anything like what you call "frenzy" ought to be suspected and resisted.

19. *"Set your teeth and hold on."*

Will it be any help to you to learn that I know many who suffer as you do? Hence I can perfectly understand what you are going through; the disgust for everything spiritual, the almost hatred of God, and the mad longing almost to leave it all behind and run away. However we know that such a step would not end the trouble or bring relief in any form; on the contrary, that would simply mean playing into the devil's hands and could only lead to one thing in the end. We know also that these trials come from God and that if one is only patient, they will pass. Hence, my dear child, you must set your teeth and hold on; spiritual life, remember, is a warfare and you will surely not run away when the real attack comes, but rather boldly face the enemy.

20.

Go, stand by the graveside of one whom you have dearly loved, and gaze for the last time upon the remains of that dear departed soul. Perhaps it is a mother whose gentle care was ever round you, whose arms were open wide that you might nestle on her bosom and tell a mother's heart your joys and childish sorrows. Well now do you recall the thousand little ways that love for you was shown, the welcome smile, the kindly word, the soft kiss implanted on your cheek. But she is dead! Those lips are cold and clammy now, and never more will you read in those glassy eyes the burning fire of love. Happy man if you can stand by that open grave and think that never by word or deed have you pained the heart of that mother lying still in death.

21. *Bugbears.*

Remember the devil is a bad spiritual director, and you may always recognise his apparently good suggestions by the disturbances they cause in the soul. Our Lord would never urge you to turn away from a path which is leading you nearer to Himself, nor frighten you with the prospect of future unbearable trials. If they do come, grace will come also and make you abound with joy in all your tribulations.

22. *Christ's Prayer.*

The life of Jesus was a continual prayer. Even during His public life He began, continued and ended everything He did by prayer, besides devoting whole nights and days to communing with His Father.

If we want our work for souls to be fruitful, we must bring prayer into it. If our children are not all that they ought to be, the cause may not be far to seek. Let us examine if we are praying enough for them, if our aspirations are ever ascending to the throne of God, to bless our work amongst those children and amongst others with whom we have to deal.

23. *Love for Christ.*

Even as a child I longed and prayed to be a saint. But somehow it always seemed to me as if that longing could never be realised, for I felt there was some kind of a barrier like a high wall between myself and God. What it was, I cannot say even now. But recently this obstacle appears to me to have been removed, the way is open, and I feel I love Jesus now as I never did before, or even hoped to. With this comes the conviction, so strong and consoling with so much peace and happiness, that Jesus will grant my heart's desire before I die. I dare not put on paper what I feel, even if I could; but at times Jesus seems to pour all the grace of His Sacred Heart upon me, until I am intoxicated almost with His love and could cry out with the pain of that sweet wounding.

24. *The Morning of Life.*

There is no more important moment in the life of a young boy or girl than when he stands with trembling feet at the parting of the ways. The days of irresponsible childhood are gone for ever, and now he must launch his bark on the stormy waters of life and steer his course for eternity. It is a solemn moment, a time big with possibilities for good or evil, for the youth is face to face with the question what he must do with his future life, a choice upon which not merely his happiness on earth, but even his eternal salvation, may depend.

25. *Practical Holiness.*

What is my special end, for which God made me? More and more each retreat I see what this is, always the same thought, always the same desire and longing for *holiness.* God wants sanctity from me. This is to be acquired chiefly by three means: (1) constant little acts of mortification; (2) constant aspirations; (3) perfection of each action, even the odd Hail Marys.

26. *Conquer Yourself.*

Vince teipsum. This is the secret of the Exercises. "I learnt no other lesson from my master Ignatius," said St. Francis Xavier, referring to his first retreat at Paris. Here we all fail - good men, zealous men, holy men. Prayer is easy, works of zeal attractive; but going against self, till grace and perseverance give facility, is cruel work, a hard battle.

27. *Walk before you run.*

Possibly you have been a little too generous in the time of fervour and have attempted more than you were able for, which would account in part, at least, for the feeling of "being crushed." However you should have been prepared to find that the generous spirit which carried you along from sacrifice to sacrifice was not intended to last, it was only meant to strengthen you for the time of trial. To serve God generously when the music of consolation is sounding in our ears is no doubt pleasing to Him, but to be equally faithful when all is black and dark is not only a thousand times more sanctifying, but is heroic virtue. Hence God, in His eagerness for our perfection takes away, at times, all sensible con solation, yet is really nearer to us than before.

The great danger to be faced is that one feels inclined to lose heart, to be discouraged - "the devil's pet walking stick" - and in the end to give up all striving for perfection, aiming only at being content with that curse of every religious house - Mediocrity.

As I said before, my dear child, I fancy you tried to do too much, to be too generous. Do not try to run till you can walk well. Draw up a list of certain little sacrifices which you feel God is asking from you and which you know you will be able to give Him without very much difficulty better be cowardly than too generous. Then, come what may, be faithful to your list and shake it in the face of the tempter when he suggests that you should give it up. After some time, when greater facility has come by practice, you might add a little to what you did at first, and so on till, please God, one day you will be able to say, "I know only Jesus Christ, and Him crucified; with Christ I am nailed to the Cross." – *I. Cor.* 2. 2; *Galat.* 2. 19.

28.

The saints had ever a childlike confidence and trust in God. Upon Him they cast all their anxieties and cares, under His powerful protection they sheltered themselves, and with His almighty help they were ever strong. They lived in the present day alone, striving to bear with cheerful hearts the burden of the moment; the morrow's work would bring its stream of graces to help them on their journey.

29. *Union is Will-Blending.*

I understand what you mean by wishing for the Mystic Union or Espousals, not that you presume to think that God will give you the special favours of the saints, but that it may be a source of greater love and grace to you. Since every little increase of sanctifying grace means also an increase of God's love for you and yours for Him, there is no harm, quite the contrary, in wishing and praying for anything that will help to that end. As regards this union with our Lord, it is really nothing more than a blending of our will with His in such a way that we wish only what He wishes and as far as possible only think of and interest ourselves in those things that are His.

30. *Hunt the "little foxes."*

It is scarcely necessary to state that deliberate sin in any shape or form utterly destroys the interior life and even gives a loathing and disgust for its practice. It is not so evident that deliberate imperfections, and for religious repeated violation of rule, have the same result. These are the "little foxes," attractive and apparently harmless creatures, which must be hunted down and destroyed, says the wise man, if the vineyard is not to perish. A soul given to sin or consciously violating the rules to which it has freely bound itself for life, will sigh in vain for the secret loving embraces of its Beloved.

[1] Imitation of Christ iii. 17, 1.

December

1. *A Common Religious Malady.*

You seem to be suffering, my dear child, from a very common religious malady discouragement and want of patience with yourself, looking for and expecting to *see* great results from your efforts to become holier. You forget what a clog the body is on the soul, and how in spite of the most generous intentions and determination, it prevents us, time after time, from carrying out our plans. You remember St. Paul's bitter com plaint that the good he wished to do he did not: "I am delighted with the law of God, but I see another law in my members, fighting against the law of my mind and captivating me in the law of sin." This is the experience of all who are striving to serve God well. They cannot always do what they would like and what they know He asks of them, but in the end the grace of God S. Paul's remedy will bring the victory, if only we persevere.

2. *Some Resolutions of Father Doyle*
(Feast of S. Stanislaus, 1907.)
My ideal: the Third Degree of Humility in all its perfection.
My great devotion: the Sacred Heart in the Blessed Eucharist.
I will say as much of my Office as I can in the chapel.
I will try and bear little sufferings without seeking relief.
Never to give way to sleep during the day.
Great attention to the Rules of Modesty, especially custody of the eyes.
To read these resolutions once a week.
Motto: *Agere contra* all for the love of Jesus and to win His love.

3. *S. Francis Xavier.*

Xavier's hour has come, the hour of his eternal reward and never-ending bliss. In a little hut, open on all sides to the biting blast, the great Apostle lies dying. Far from home and all that makes this life pleasant, far from the quiet of his own religious house, alone upon this barren isle, our Saint will yield his soul to God. What joy fills his heart now at the thought of the sacrifices he has made, the honours he has despised, the pleasures left behind. Happy sufferings! Happy penances! He thinks of what his life might have been, the life of a gay worldling, and in gratitude he lifts his eyes to thank his God for the graces given him. What matter now the hardships he has endured? All, all, are past, for now the sweet reward of heaven is inviting him to his eternal rest.

4. *The Incarnation.*

By her simple "fiat" Mary brought to pass the most wondrous miracle of all time. In silent expectation the Heavenly Court had watched the great Archangel speed on his way towards the humble home of Nazareth. With joy they heard the virgin's humble words of meek submission which brought the Maker of the world to dwell within her womb, and now they see their God, the great God of all creatures dwelling as a little babe among sinful men.

What must have been Mary's thoughts when first she felt the infant child within her womb, and realised that from her pure blood He had fashioned to Himself a human form? She His Mother He her Son! What sweet converse between the two, what words of love, of ardent, tender love, the promptings of a heart so pure and good and holy.

5. *God in Everything.*

I want you to make a greater effort to see the hand of God in *everything* that happens, and then to force or train yourself to rejoice in His holy will. For example, you want a fine day for some reason and it turns out wet. Don't say, "Oh, hang it!" but give our Lord a loving smile and say: "Thank You, my God, for this disappointment." This will help you to keep down impatience, irritability, etc., when people annoy you. Then when some hard trial is past, look back on it, see how you ought to have taken it, and resolve to act that way in future.

6. *Give God His time.*

You must trust entirely in our Lord. He alone can help you. Devote study-time to earnest work and then forget all about it. Give God His time. Be generous with Him and He will be so with you. Make frequent aspirations and keep silence this last is of the utmost importance. Your presence in the choir at meditation is a great act of faith; if you cannot pray, just think of Him who is present before you. If ever you leave this holy house, it will be your own fault. If you are faithful to God He will place His loving arms around you and hold you tight. Put away all fear in this regard; a soul in fear cannot be united to God. Trust, trust, trust. God gave you a vocation; He does not do things by halves.

7. *Interior Penance.*

I believe strongly in corporal penance as a means to the end. But a denial of your own will often costs more than a hundred strokes of the discipline. To interior penance you need not, and must not, put any limit.

8. *Mary's Sinlessness.*

God delights to honour His saints by bestowing upon them special graces which mark them off from the rest of mankind. To one He gives a burning zeal for souls; to another the thirst for suffering and humiliation, but on Mary alone He bestowed the supreme privilege of freedom from the taint of sin.

From the first moment of her conception till she closed her eyes forever on this world, Mary was undefiled, unspotted by the least taint of sin. Never for an instant did the fierce and fiery burst of temptation ruffle the calm of her holy soul; for her the forbidden pleasures of this life, for which man will barter his priceless soul, had no false attraction. Sin might rage around her, hell might move its mighty depths, but nought could tarnish the spotless beauty of her who was to be the Mother of God.

9.

The desire to be a saint has been growing in my heart all during this year, especially the last couple of months. God has given me this desire; He will not refuse the grace, if only I am faithful in the future. How good you have been to me, O my God, waiting so patiently for me to return to You! Help me now generously to do all You want me to do.

10. *Refuse Him Nothing.*

I want to be generous with God and to refuse Him nothing. I do not want to say, "I will go just so far and no farther." Hence I feel my cowardly and weak nature dreading this retreat, for I feel our Lord is going to ask some big sacrifice from me, that He expects much from me. He has been tugging at my heart for so many years, urging me in so many ways to give myself wholly to Him, to give all and refuse Him nothing. I dread lest now I shall again refuse Him - perhaps it is the last time He will ask me to do what He wants. My loving Jesus, I will, I *will* be generous with You now at last. But You must aid me, it must be Your work, I am so cowardly. Make me see clearly Your holy will.

11.

I am sorry to see you suffer and yet glad that the cross is your portion. If I had at this moment the gift of miracles, I would not cure you, I should be afraid the cross is far too precious to take away from anyone. Do not seek to rid yourself of it, rather love it, embrace it, and will to have it, because God wills it for you.

12. *Abandonment.*

To-day at Exposition I asked our Lord to let me know what He wished you to correct especially during your retreat. It seems to me, my child, that most of your faults come from a want of perfect abandonment to the will of God. For example, when you get annoyed with people and speak sharply, you lose sight of God's directing hand, which prompted or allowed people to act in this way. God's will is constantly clashing with ours, and unless a soul is perfectly sub missive, interior peace is disturbed or lost. True abandonment means crushing out self and welcoming with sweetness and joy all God sends.

13. *Do not be uneasy.*

As long as the desire of pleasing God remains in your heart and there is a steady constant effort towards perfection, you need never be uneasy about your state of soul. Everything else, small imperfections and even deliberate faults, coldness in prayer, are mere details in a life which is very pleasing to God. Do not expect to see much progress, but rest assured that the advance is certain and steady. Get more prayer into your life, if you can.

14. *Childlike Trust.*

Surely you are not right in trying to keep our Lord away from you, or in thinking that He looks upon you with displeasure. When sin in the past is repented for, the poor soul who once strayed from Him has a strange attraction for His gentle Heart. You pain Him intensely if you think He does not love you now, nor wish for your affection. Give Him all you can, warmly and naturally, like a little child, and rest assured that the one longing of His Heart is to see you advance rapidly in holiness and perfection. You must try and cultivate great confidence and trust in our dear Lord's love and mercy, driving far from you sadness and regret of all kinds. Give it no quarter, it is all from the devil and so most harmful.

15. *Want of Will.*

A want of will is the chief obstacle to our becoming saints. We are not holy because we do not really wish to become so. We would indeed gladly possess the virtues of the saints their humility and patience, their love of suffering, their penance and zeal. But we are unwilling to embrace all that goes to make a saint and to enter on the narrow path which leads to sanctity. A strong will, a resolute will, is needed; a will which is not to be broken by difficulties or turned aside by trifling obstacles; a determination to be a saint and not to faint and falter because the way seems long and hard and narrow. A big heart, a courageous heart, is needed for sanctification, to fight our worst enemy our own self-love.

16. *The Gift of Time.*

God has many gifts to bestow upon us, but none more precious than time. Yet how we abuse this royal gift! How little we think of it! How we despise these golden moments, moments whose true value we shall not really prize till alas! too late - when time shall be no more for us.

17. *A "Football."*

Don t lose sight of this principle, that true holiness is based on humility which can never be attained except by humiliations and plenty of them. Pray daily that "the hard knocks of humiliation" may increase, for holiness will grow in proportion. Do not forget, with reference to what you have to suffer from others, that it is all part of God's plan for your sanctification. If you want to be a saint, you must suffer, and in the way that pleases God, not yourself. Till you come to recognize that you are a "football" and really deserve to be kicked by everyone, the grace of God will not produce its effect in your soul. "He hath regarded the humility of His handmaid." - *S. Luke* 1. 48.

18.

"I have called upon Thee in the day of my trouble." *Psalm* 85. 7. Jesus is our comforter. What burden is there which He cannot lighten? What cross that He cannot make sweet? Be our troubles what they may, if only we will call on Jesus and implore His aid, we shall find our sufferings lessened and the rough ways smoothed for our bleeding feet.

19. *Graces Lost by Missing One Communion.*

1. The visit to our soul of Jesus the Author of every grace and all holiness.
2. Increase of sanctifying grace.
3. Sacramental grace which gives the right to actual graces when needed to avoid sin, discharge duties of state, etc.
4. Remission of every venial sin.
5. Remission of mortal sin if forgotten.
6. Preservative from sin: extinguished fire of passion.
7. Entire or partial remission of temporal punishment.

8. Spiritual joy and sweetness.

9. Special glory of the body at the Resurrection.

10. Merit greater degree of glory.

11. Indulgences lost: *En ego.* Possible graces lost. In one Communion lost through one's own fault may depend:

1. Complete victory over a fault or a passion. **2.** Some particular grace long prayed for. **3.** Conversion, salvation of some soul. **4.** Deliverance of a soul in Purgatory. **5.** Graces for others.

20.

There is no rule for vocations, no age-limit for the Call. Innocence attracts the gaze of God, deep-rooted habits of sin, provided they are not persevered in, do not always repel Him. One conies because the world disgusts him, another loves it and leaves it with regret; docility draws down more graces, while resistance often increases the force of the invitation. The little child hears God's whisperings, while others have not been summoned till years were far advanced.

21.

Jesus is very gentle but very firm with me. He has shown me that I must not shrink from what He wants. He is ever near urging me in the same direction; you know where His divine face was turned so constantly during life and at its close. I am not afraid of sacrifice; He has given me a most intense love for suffering and humiliation, but why, oh why, did He make me so wretchedly weak that I cannot take one step if His strong arm is not around me?

22. *Definite Practical Resolutions.*

Reading over my reflections and resolutions on the Third Degree during the Long Retreat, I see now they are little more than empty promises; they have produced no real change in my life. I put before myself "always to choose the hard thing, to go against self in all things." But have I really done so since? Has my life been more mortified from the time I made this resolution? Now, however, I am fully resolved no longer to "beat the air," but have drawn up a list of definite acts of self-denial by which I can test myself. If only I am faithful to these, I shall indeed have begun to lead a new and better life than formerly.

23. *The Prayer of Christ.*

"He went out into a mountain to pray; and He passed the whole night in the prayer of God." - *Luke* 6. 12.

Christ prays, on His knees, humbly, reverently. I watch Him well during this great act of His life. Lord, teach me how to pray like You.

He goes up into a mountain, away from all that may distract Him. He leaves His preaching, His work, even the thought of it, behind. In quiet and solitude He goes on His knees, humbly as a creature, reverently as a child.

He had gone through a long hard day's work, He was weary, longing for rest and sleep. Yet He passed the *whole* night in the prayer of God. To teach me the need of prayer, to teach me to love prayer, to teach me to persevere in prayer.

24.

"All our days are spent." - *Psalm* 89. 9. The hour will come for each of us when we shall echo these words of the Psalmist, when with anxious eyes we shall watch the last few sands of our life run out for ever. What avail then will be our useless regrets that we have made such little use of those precious days? Will our bitter sorrow and biting remorse bring back even one of the moments we have so uselessly squandered in idle pleasure or consumed in sinful deeds?

25. *The Nativity.*

What impressed me most in the meditation on the Nativity was the thought that Jesus could have been born in wealth and luxury, or at least with the ordinary comforts of life, but He chose all that was hard, unpleasant and uncomfortable. This He did *for me,* to show me the life I must lead *for Him.* If I want to be with Christ, I must lead the life of Christ, and in that life there was little of what was pleasing to nature. I think I have been following Christ, yet how pleasant and comfortable my life has always been ever avoiding cold, hunger, hard work, disagreeable things, humiliations, etc. My Jesus, You are speaking to my heart now. I cannot mistake Your voice or hide from myself what You want from me and what my future life should be. Help me for I am weak and cowardly.

26. *The Worldly Spirit.*

Christ Himself has openly declared that He is not of this world, neither is His spirit to be found there. Hence the fruits of the interior life will not be found in a soul which seeks delight in the pleasures and amusements of worldlings, who devour the papers for the latest news or can lose themselves in the pages of a novel; who are ever seeking for all that gratifies the senses; heedless of the fact that all these worldly images come crowding back into the mind when the moment of prayer arrives and are constantly driving away the thought of God - the true food of the soul aspiring to perfection far away.

Under this heading may be placed all friend ships which are not centred in God, for He is a jealous God and will not have our heart divided with any creature.

27.

One Victory out of ten Opportunities. Thank God you are keeping up the good fight against self. But Don't get into your head that this battle ought to be easy, it is fearfully hard. The devil knows it well and so he tries to dis courage one altogether by fixing our attention on what we do *not* do, in order to hide our generosity from us. If you gain one victory out of every ten opportunities, you ought to be well satisfied; certainly our Blessed Lord is, because He knows our weakness better than we do.

28.

Every little victory in the matter of food is a real triumph, for this is a real test of generosity. You will find many persons given to prayer, works of zeal, penance, but most seem to fly from the denial of their appetite; my health, Father; the greater glory of God, etc. St. Francis de Sales used to say, "Unless you deny your appetite, you will never be a saint" a mighty saying!

All the same, my child, I think it would please our Lord more, at this Christmas season of joy, to relax a little and even indulge the body. It will help you to renew the fight later with more energy.

29.

How miserable has been my service of God since I entered religion! A bit fervent one day, the next dissipated and careless, even since my ordination. I have fallen away from the fervent way in which I resolved to live henceforth. I feel inclined to despond; but with God's help I will go on, trying now at last to make some little progress in serving Him worthily. My true service of God consists in performing the ordinary actions of the day as perfectly and as fervently as I can, with a pure intention for love of my Jesus. It is a mistake to think that I can only serve Him by preaching, saving souls, etc. What would have become of me if I had treated an earthly master as I have served God?

30.

Our Lord is often as much pleased (more, S. Teresa says) by our good intentions and desires than by their execution. The good desire, the longing and wish to be perfect, is strong in you, and as long as that remains you need never fear displeasing God. Besides, you have a tremendous lever of sanctification in the power of love that enables us to do things, especially what costs us an effort, for our Lord's dear sake. Mind, this, does not mean feeling, sensible affection, but simply a dry act of the will, intending to make the sacrifice or action an act of pure love. "My God, I do this for the love of You, and for no one else in the world would I do it." Try this in easy things, and occasionally make a dive at a really big sacrifice which costs, for love means sacrifice, and sacrifice leads infallibly to love.

31. *Avoid Worry.*

Avoid worry, anxiety, uneasiness about any thing. With good people this takes the form of doubt about past confessions or of salvation. "The devil's boiling pot" expresses this state of mind; one trouble ended, another crops up to take its place; the soul never at rest; there is no peace, no calm, and also no real holiness.

Anxiety about success or failure of enterprises is another common form of worry. This comes from the remains of self-love which has not been completely rooted out, and from secret pride which rebels against failure even when God wishes it, and against the consequent humiliation. This anxiety and fear show also the want of perfect conformity to God's will which is the groundwork of perfect peace of soul.